READING
THE
STARS

READING THE STARS

ASTROLOGY
for
BOOK LOVERS

Book Riot

Abrams Image, New York

CONTENTS

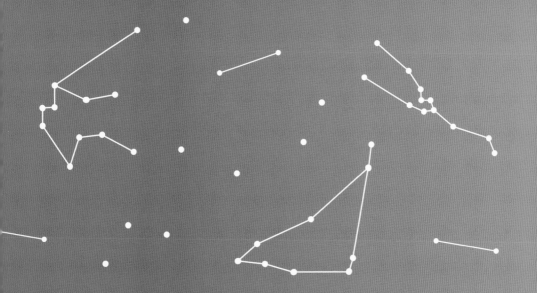

INTRODUCTION

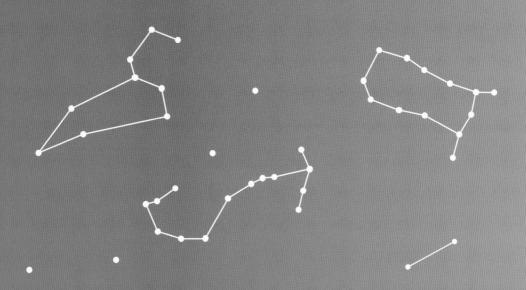

Welcome to the wonderful world of bookish astrology! This book is intended to help you better understand the planets, their impact on you, and how your zodiac sign shapes your reading life. Astrology can help inform how you previece yourself and others, can provide guidance for your relationships, and may even be helpful while choosing a cocktail at happy hour! And like other aspects of life, reading is equally important and equally open to growth and change.

But before we get there, it's helpful to have a basic understanding of astrology and your own zodiac signs. Yes, signs—plural!

Astrology has a long, winding history, dating back more than four thousand years to ancient Babylonia. Today, astrologers have a variety of approaches to interpreting celestial movements, but they share the belief that we can be deeply impacted and shaped by the universe in ways we can't always see. And, inspired by the planets' journeys around the sun, astrology recognizes that cyclical patterns and repetition can teach us a lot about the world around us.

Learning about your astrological placements can give you a helpful window into your own inner workings, which can in turn help you discover new things to bring you joy and support your personal growth. Since you're here, we're guessing you like books, yes? Well, astrology can certainly give you some hints about what kind of books you like to read, what books can help you grow as a person, and how you engage with the reading world.

We'll start off with a little background on the key concepts of astrology, what shapes the signs of the zodiac, and how the signs interact with each other. After that, we'll discuss each of the signs in more detail and explore how each sign reads.

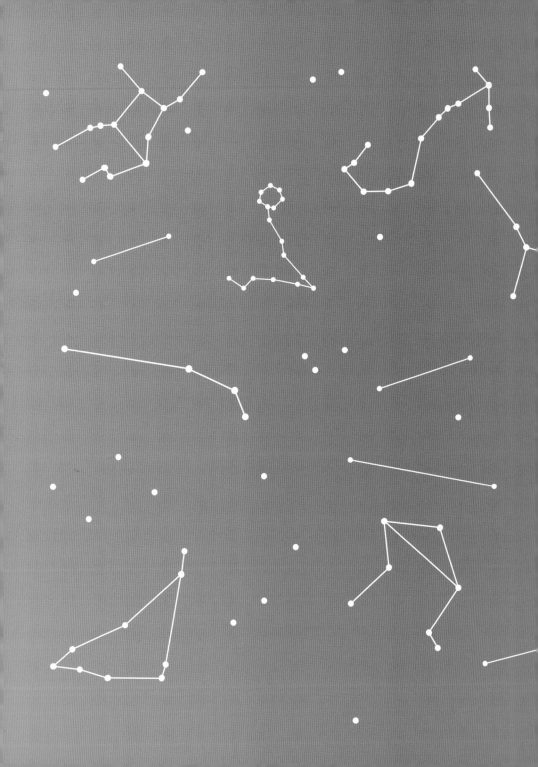

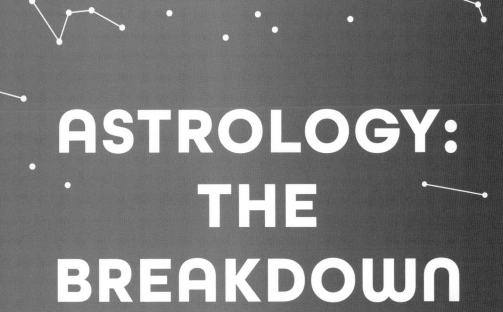

ASTROLOGY:
THE
BREAKDOWN

Sun and Moon and Rising Signs, Oh My!

When someone walks up to you at a bar and says, "Hey, baby, what's your sign?" they're probably asking about your sun sign. But while your sun sign says a lot about you, astrology isn't quite as simple as sorting everyone into the twelve signs and calling it a day. Your astrological placements come in many packages, with each house and planet making up another part of your magical, mystical being. Generally, you can get a pretty good idea of what makes someone tick if you know their sun sign, moon sign, and rising sign. All three are determined by the movement of the planets at the exact date, time, and location of your birth. The fastest way to identify your signs is by using one of the many free birth-chart calculators online. Go ahead and look your birth chart up now. Don't worry, we'll wait.

Alright, now that you know your sun, moon, and rising signs, what do they mean? Let's start with your sun sign, the one you probably already knew before you picked up this book. When you see a range of dates associated with a sign, it's referencing your sun sign, associated broadly with the day of your birth. Your sun sign is the most influential sign for your identity, the one that generally makes up your personality, habits, and instincts. If you read horoscopes, look at the listing for your sun sign for a broad view of how planetary movements may impact you. When it comes to your reading life, think of your sun sign as what influences your all-time favorite books and genres.

If you were born within a couple of days of the switchover between two signs, that makes you a cusper. Because the planets were shifting from one station to another when you were born, you may find that you have qualities from the signs on either side. This is a bit of a blessing and a curse; having qualities from two signs gives you greater perspective and versatility, but it may also cause some inner conflict when your two sun signs clash.

Your moon sign is the sign that guides your internal life, like how you behave while you're alone or how you interact with your closest friends and family. It's the part of your personality that not everyone sees but is still intimately connected to how you understand and approach the world. Knowing your moon sign can help you better understand how you interact emotionally with your loved ones and where you turn for relaxation and security. Think of your moon sign as determining your comfort books, the ones you read solely for your own enjoyment.

Quite the opposite, your rising sign determines how you present yourself to the world. It influences how you want to be perceived by others or how you shape your personal brand. While it's helpful to understand your instincts when it comes to public appearances, it's not necessarily as important for your interiority as your sun and moon signs. Think of your rising sign as the books you read to impress other people rather than out of genuine interest—or perhaps the books you artistically pose and photograph for Instagram but have yet to actually read.

Understanding the Elements: Reading Styles

If you're new to astrology, you may have trouble remembering the differences between the twelve zodiac signs. A helpful way to understand the different signs, and especially how they interact with each other, is to consider their elements. Each sign falls under one of four elements: fire, earth, air, and water. The pattern of elements repeats through the signs in that order, starting with the fire sign Aries.

Knowing someone's element can give you a general idea of their priorities, values, and view of the world, though it's not definitive. There's much more to everyone than their astrological sign, and within each sign there's plenty of room for variation. Think of the elements as a general rule or guiding principle, rather than a finite system that everyone fits into perfectly.

Fire signs include Aries, Leo, and Sagittarius. They're united by their fiery, competitive spirit and independent streaks. At their best, fire signs are passionate, adventurous, and energetic. At their most difficult, they can be impulsive, combative, and egotistical. Fire signs tend toward ambitious reading goals and reading for sport instead of pleasure. They also like to see themselves in a protagonist, and seek out stories accordingly.

Earth signs include Taurus, Virgo, and Capricorn. They are traditionalists at heart who value rules, family, and earthly pleasures. The world is mostly black-and-white to earth signs, with little room for any gray area. At their best, earth signs are responsible, patient, and loyal. At their most difficult, they can be hard-headed, predictable, and a bit lazy. Earth signs are the most likely to limit themselves to only one or two genres and love rereading old favorites. They dislike ambiguous endings, preferring books with a clean finish.

Air signs include Gemini, Libra, and Aquarius. They are constantly learning, and their curiosity, intellect, and communication skills make them highly social. On a good day, air signs are charming, creative, and engaging. On a bad day, they're distant, indecisive, and volatile. Air signs read everything because they want to know everything. They look for new perspectives in books across multiple genres, usually enjoying more than one at a time.

Water signs include Cancer, Scorpio, and Pisces. They have a deep understanding of and connection to emotions, making them highly perceptive and sensitive. On a good day, water signs are expressive, intuitive, and romantic. On a bad day, they're mercurial, melancholic, and dramatic. When it comes to reading, water signs prefer emotionally intense, character-driven narratives. They tend to appreciate poetry more than the other elements.

Pending your rising, sun, and moon signs, and how strongly your personality identifies with your astrological element, you'll likely see some of the tendencies in your own reading interests. Or perhaps if you don't, they can guide you as you look for new books and authors to explore!

The Qualities: In a Book Club

The signs can also be categorized by three different "qualities," or ways of approaching their environments and communities. These qualities often come into play in social situations, and when important decisions need to be made. The qualities are cardinal, fixed, and mutable, and they also follow that repeating pattern through the signs, starting with cardinal Aries.

Cardinal signs include Aries, Cancer, Libra, and Capricorn. They generally have strong opinions on how things should go and prefer being in control. They're natural leaders who enjoy new challenges. In a book club, a cardinal sign is the one who organizes and leads the meetings.

Fixed signs include Taurus, Leo, Scorpio, and Aquarius. They like to mind their own business, and would prefer if you would do the same. They avoid change, preferring to stick with what they know. In a book club, they push back against book choices outside their comfort zones.

Mutable signs include Gemini, Virgo, Sagittarius, and Pisces. Typically laid-back, they are easily influenced by those around them and don't mind going with the flow. They are open to new experiences without needing to control them. In a book club, they'll go with whatever the group chooses.

Planetary Rule

As you go deeper into astrology, you'll find that everything is determined by the movement of the planets. Your birth chart includes a sign for each planet, and you can spend hours exploring how they work together to create the beautiful, unique being that is you. But each zodiac sign is also ruled by a planet, or in some cases, two planets. Your sun sign's ruling planet helps determine your energy and drive.

You can learn a lot about your ruling planet simply by understanding the Roman god after whom it was named. The qualities and personality traits typically assigned to that god have something in common with your sign. For example, Mars is named after the Roman god of war, often associated with passion, aggression, and ambition. Aries, ruled by Mars, is known for its fiery spirit and competitive nature. Saturn, named for the Roman god of agriculture, rules Capricorn and instills it with a sense of discipline, hard work, and a desire for growth.

Some signs have two ruling planets, with one functioning as the primary ruler and the other as a secondary ruler. For example, Pisces is primarily ruled by Neptune, named for the Roman god of the sea, contributing to the dreamy, artistic, and sensitive nature of those whose sun sign is Pisces. Secondarily, Pisces is ruled by Jupiter, king of the gods, giving Pisces leadership skills and a touch of good luck.

Don't let the name deceive you; some signs' ruling planets aren't planets at all. Leo's "ruling planet" is the sun, matching Leos' desire to be at the center of everything. The sun brings Leo a certain magnetism, vitality, and confidence. Cancer is ruled by the moon, which you may recall from learning about moon signs determines our emotions and most intimate selves. This is why Cancers are considered to be deeply sensitive, nurturing, and in touch with their feelings.

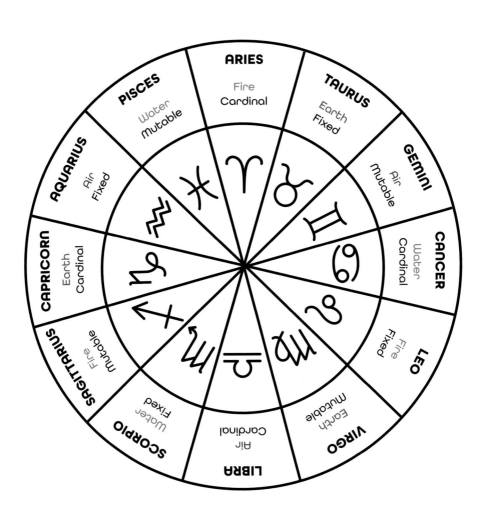

The Zodiac Circle of Life

Traditionally, Aries is considered the first sign of the zodiac, followed by Taurus, Gemini, Cancer, and the rest of the signs, all the way through Pisces. The signs are often displayed in a wheel like the one opposite.

This wheel is a helpful image to understand the patterns and repetition of the signs. The order of the signs is also important when considering the metaphorical "age" of each sign. This circle represents a full life cycle, with each sign representing a point in life. Keep in mind that these ages are not at all literal; they're more of a way to understand the signs' views on life and energy, like someone being "young at heart" or "an old soul."

Aries are the newborns of the zodiac, full of energy and excitement, ready to take on the world but perhaps a bit naive. Cancers are mid-childhood, guided by their changing moods and instincts and are closely tied to their families. Libras are twentysomethings, working hard, concerned with what others think, and starting to find their place in the world. Capricorns are nearing retirement age, confident and capable, if a bit stuck in their ways. And Pisces are metaphorically at the end of life, with all the wisdom and emotional intelligence of their years.

When it comes to reading, your metaphorical age may have some impact on the books that most resonate with you. Those with earlier signs in the zodiac may feel especially connected to their favorite books from childhood or appreciate the creativity and curiosity of children's books. Those with signs in the southeast corner of the wheel may be especially drawn to young adult and new adult books. And those with signs toward the end of the zodiac may have started reading books way above their maturity level at a young age.

Can't We All Just Get Along?

People often look to astrology to help them figure out with whom they are and aren't compatible. While astrology certainly isn't the be-all and end-all of compatibility, the planets can give us a useful understanding of others. A few tips for discovering what signs you may jive with best are below, but keep in mind that relationships can (and do!) exist outside of astrological compatibility. Those relationships may just require a little more work and communication to understand how you approach the world differently.

Generally speaking, you'll find it pretty easy to understand people with the same sign as you, although too much similarity can sometimes be a bad thing. You'll also get along pretty well with other signs of your element. For example, Sagittarius, Leo, and Aries share certain fire sign qualities that help them hit it off. But some of the best relationships come from the two element pairings that appropriately balance each other: air with fire, and water with earth. Air signs bring a detached thoughtfulness to fire signs' passion and drive, and vice versa. Earth signs' grounded, level-headed nature balances water signs' emotion and intuition. The air-fire and water-earth groupings are a helpful general rule to understand what signs do and don't naturally get along.

The qualities are another tool for understanding how different signs interact. Remember that cardinal signs prefer to lead, mutable signs like to follow, and fixed signs want to be left alone. Mutable signs are fairly compatible with any quality, but cardinal and fixed signs may often find themselves bumping heads.

Consider also the wheel image on page 14. Where other signs fall in relation to yours can help you better understand your compatibility. The signs directly before and after you, which are the two elements you relate to the least, are signs you struggle to understand. That doesn't mean you won't like anyone with those signs; you just see the world through different lenses. However, the signs on either side of those, two signs before and after yours, are highly compatible with you. They both represent the element that balances you best. Signs directly across the wheel from each other, for example, Taurus and Scorpio, share a unique bond. They have similar goals and visions of the world, but go about reaching them in completely opposite ways. Signs across the wheel may be passionately drawn to each other, but their disagreements may be just as passionate.

Dangit, Is Mercury in Retrograde Again?

There are many planetary oddities noted in astrology, but none garners the same reputation and sense of dread as Mercury retrograde. You may hear people blame Mercury retrograde whenever things go wrong in their lives, and while it's not always at fault, it's definitely caused many a ruckus.

So what does it mean? Mercury is in retrograde when it appears to be moving in reverse from our position on Earth, an optical illusion caused by how much more quickly Mercury circles the sun than does the Earth. Mercury retrograde occurs about three to four times a year, usually lasting about three weeks.

Mercury, named after the Roman messenger to the gods, rules communication, travel, and technology. So when Mercury is in retrograde, you're likely to see its negative impacts when it comes to those areas of your life. Scheduling mix-ups, cancelled flights, buggy technology, and misunderstandings may be more common during this time. Keep in mind that the strongest effects occur in the few days leading up to Mercury retrograde, and in the few days after it returns to apparent forward motion.

It's hard to avoid the problems Mercury retrograde may introduce in your life, but the best thing you can do is check, double-check, and check one more time on anything relating to travel, technology, or communication. It's also important to keep a cool head during disagreements and clarify as much as possible to avoid confusion. Our best advice to avoid Mercury retrograde chaos? Stay home and read a book.

Is Astrology Real?

If you've made it to this point in the book and you're still a skeptic, first off, you're probably an earth sign. A Taurus, maybe? If I'm wrong, check your moon sign.

Regardless of how much you buy into astrology, you can absolutely take something away from what it teaches us about the world, and you can usually have some fun along the way. Because astrology is tied to the planets, it requires a basic knowledge of the galaxy, which can come in handy. There's also a lot of history and mythology tied up in astrology, making it even more interesting to explore.

But most of all, it's a way of exploring how we relate to the world and the people around us. When considering the vast universe and the effects of planetary motion on our personal lives, we're forced to look at life through a wider lens. Astrology is built on the concept that each of us is a complicated and unique combination of personality traits, skills, worries, and passions. All of us, much like the night sky, are so much more than we appear to be. Astrology is sometimes accused of simply dividing people into twelve vaguely described buckets, but as you've read already, astrology goes much further than your sun sign. It recognizes that there are a million things, often conflicting, that make you the person you are, and the same is true for everyone else around you.

If you love someone, comparing your charts is an intimate way to explore how you interact with each other. And if you have a difficult relationship with someone, perhaps the planets can give you a common language to help you explore why you struggle to see eye to eye. Much like enneagrams, psychological personality inventories, *Dungeons & Dragons* alignments, and your favorite online "Which Golden Girl Are You?" quiz, astrology is a way to explore the things that make us different and gives us a window into how to overcome those differences. If nothing else, consider it an exercise in empathy.

And like it or hate it, astrology is here to stay. It arrived on Earth long before you, and it will be here long after you leave. So you might as well get that sun sign—inspired tattoo we know you've been considering!

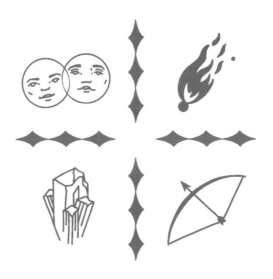

HOW TO USE THIS BOOK

There are many ways to use this book, just as there are many ways to incorporate astrology into your life. Whether you know your birth chart by heart, check your horoscope every now and then, or are just beginning to learn about astrology, *Reading the Stars* is for you. Like books, astrology is a lens through which to make sense of the world and your place in it. So why not add another tool to help along your journey through life?

Start by using this book as a means to gain insight and for personal growth. As you develop an understanding of the major components of your star chart and their connections to your personality, you'll begin to see your relationships in new ways and approach life with greater clarity. Use the reading recommendations for your sun, moon, and rising signs to help you build your strengths and explore areas of self-improvement. And if you have loved ones who are into astrology, you'll be able to use the common language of the stars to deepen those relationships, too.

And of course, books make great gifts! Buy a copy of *Reading the Stars* to do a book-club read with a friend, or use it as a jumping-off point for finding great books to give as gifts. Have a Sagittarius friend who loves to travel? Flip to the Sagittarius section of the library to find some books that will stoke their sense of adventure.

Finally, you can use this book to better understand your favorite writers. We've included a few famous writers born under each sign. If your fave isn't on the list, simply look up their birthdate, read about their sign, and see how it aligns with your reading of their work.

We hope you'll find *Reading the Stars* to be a fun and informative way to make your reading life—and your life in general—bigger and more meaningful.

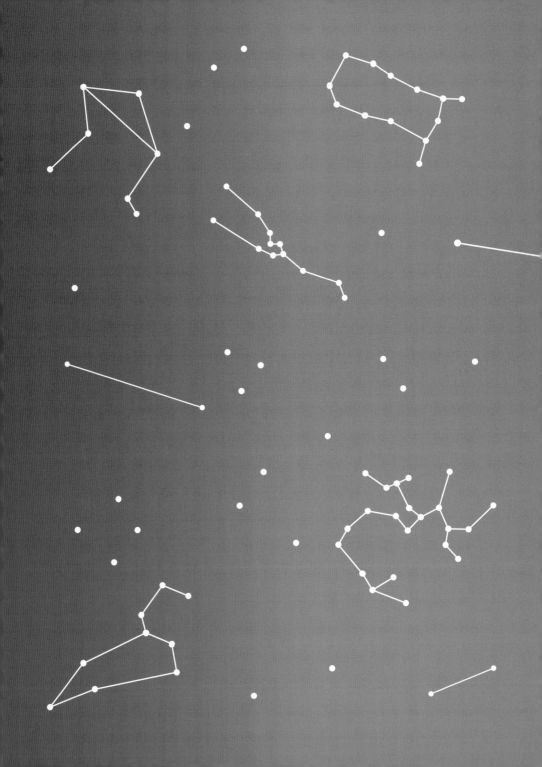

READING
THE SIGNS

Aries
(March 21–April 19)

ELEMENT: Fire
QUALITY: Cardinal
RULING PLANET: Mars
SYMBOL: The Ram

The Basics:

As any Billy Joel fan knows, no one will admit to starting the fire. But in truth, it was an Aries, the first sign of the zodiac, and they probably got away with it. Aries are the fieriest of fire signs, known for their competitive spirit, quick temper, and habit of jumping into action—sometimes without thinking very far ahead. They're symbolized by the ram, ready to go horns-first into any situation.

In the life cycle of the zodiac, Aries is a newborn, eyes wide open and ready to take on the world. And as happens with a baby, it's hard to hate an Aries, even if they get themselves into some messy situations. They're just so excited and happy to be here! Aries's positive attitude can turn any problem into a fun challenge.

An Aries will go to bat for you, but sometimes you'll have to wait while they finish the seventeen other projects they have going. Even if you haven't spoken to them in years, when you see them again, it feels like no time has passed at all. As a lover, they'll certainly keep you interested, but will rarely let you win an argument. Aries thrive in careers with clear goals and plenty of individual recognition and make great leaders—as long as they don't hold others to the same expectations they have for themselves.

Aries Reading Life:

Like much of an Aries's life, they can see reading as a competition. You've never seen someone as intense about a reading goal as an Aries. They love stories with a competitive edge or with an underdog protagonist who fights their way to the top. Because they can easily grow bored, they prefer plot-driven books and high stakes.

In the bookish world, you're most likely to find Aries doorbusting a library sale or promoting their bookstagram. They see reading as a social hobby and love book clubs, especially as an opportunity to debate other readers. Their bookshelves are full of ambitious books they hope to read some day, as soon as they get some free time. (Spoiler alert: They never will.)

Reading for Growth:

Aries can be very sore losers, so books about losing gracefully or turning failure into a learning moment are great personal development books. Books about seeing life as a journey rather than a destination can also be productive for the ram.

Literary Soulmate:

Capricorn

Aries and Capricorn tend to either love or hate each other, as their competitiveness and drive can lead either to mutual respect or to an intense rivalry. But when it comes to reading, both love nothing more than comparing the statuses of their reading goals and enormous TBR piles. Both also love a strong protagonist with something to prove.

Famous Aries Authors:

- Maya Angelou—April 4:
Whether writing poetry, autobiographies, essays, plays, movies, or television shows, with classic Aries passion, Angelou threw herself fully into every project she took on during her decades-long career.

- Beverly Cleary—April 12:
Although she was marked as a "struggling reader" in elementary school, Cleary's determination made her one of America's best-selling authors, and characters like Ramona Quimby mirror her fiery spirit.

Reading Recommendations

• *Warcross* by Marie Lu

This book combines two of the reading loves of an Aries: a fast-paced plot and a competition. Warcross is a virtual reality competition that has taken over the globe in popularity. Emika is trying to scrape together some extra cash, and she decides to take a chance by hacking into the opening ceremonies of the international Warcross championships. She's caught, but instead of being arrested, she's hired by the company to be a spy. This is a story that will capture the ram's short attention span and never let go. Make sure to have the sequel on hand!

• *Haikyu!!* series by Haruichi Furudate, translated by Adrienne Beck

The Aries is always midway through a challenge, so if they are looking to meet an astronomical Goodreads goal, manga is an excellent choice. Not only are they quick to get through, there are also tons of sports manga that will provide the competitive atmosphere an Aries thrives on. This one is about a high school volleyball team. Hinata is determined to become a great player, making up for his short stature with an impressive vertical leap. He is also forced to work with a teammate with exceptional skills but a short temper—something the ram is sure to sympathize with.

• *The Regional Office Is Under Attack!* by Manuel Gonzales

The Regional Office is an organization of super-powered female assassins defending the world from darkness. It's part superhero movie, part spy story, and all action. It also packs in a lot of humor and some gentle satire of the superhero genre. The short chapters, constant action, and world-ending stakes will keep an Aries reader glued to the page. It also juggles different perspectives and time periods, so there's always something new to keep those pages flipping. It's a romp of a read that also includes easter eggs that nod to action movies and superhero stories, which are exactly the kind of narratives an Aries can't resist.

• *How to Do Nothing: Resisting the Attention Economy* by Jenny Odell

This won't be an easy read for the Aries, who is always chasing the next source of excitement and has trouble just sitting with themselves, but that's exactly why they should consider it. Despite the title, this isn't a self-help book or an instructional guide. Instead, it's a deeply researched exploration of what is lost when our attention is constantly being pulled in a thousand directions at once, especially on social media. As the baby of the zodiac, Aries is easily distracted by the next shiny thing, but this book asks them to consider how they might deliberately portion out their time and attention.

• *Radical Acceptance: Embracing Your Life with the Heart of a Buddha* by Tara Brach

The Aries always has a new project and lofty goal in mind, which keeps them moving forward, but it can be difficult when those goals don't come to fruition. *Radical Acceptance* uses both elements of Buddhism and the author's background as a psychologist to cultivate compassion for oneself no matter the life circumstances. Meditation and mindfulness are practices that won't come easily to the impulsive Aries, but if they push through the initial resistance, these tools will allow them to live better lives when facing failure as well as success. This is a friendly primer to a topic that will be intimidating for the ram.

• *Dead Dead Girls* by Nekesa Afia

The ram needs a hook to be pulled through a novel, which makes mysteries an excellent choice. Aries are sure to take it upon themselves to try to solve a whodunit before the answer is revealed, and that built-in challenge will help keep their attention. The series of which this is the first volume has the added intrigue of taking place in 1920s Harlem. Louise is a queer Black woman trying to avoid trouble while working in a speakeasy, but she becomes a reluctant detective when several Black women go missing from the neighborhood. Her involvement might save lives, but it also puts hers in danger.

- *Four Thousand Weeks: Time Management for Mortals* by Oliver Burkeman

Aries seems to always be going at top speed, so it's worth taking a moment to recognize that no matter how good you are or how competitive you become, you can't do it all. *Four Thousand Weeks* is a reminder to focus on priorities instead of trying to become more and more productive. Set aside the to-do lists and enjoy the moment. Then start considering what you really want to do with your finite time on this planet. (Hint: It's probably not becoming the most efficient employee ever to design a color-coded spreadsheet.)

Further Reading

- *Binti* by Nnedi Okorafor
- *Dumplin'* by Julie Murphy
- *How to Live Safely in a Science Fictional Universe* by Charles Yu

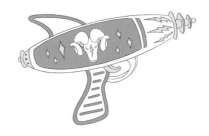

- *The Girls I've Been* by Tess Sharpe
- *The Year of the Witching* by Alexis Henderson

Taurus

(April 20–May 20)

ELEMENT: Earth
QUALITY: Fixed
RULING PLANET: Venus
SYMBOL: The Bull

The Basics:

Taurus is the steadiest and most reliable sign of the zodiac. Some may interpret those qualities as boring, but luckily, Taurus doesn't care what you think. Symbolized by the bull, Taurus is known for having a hard head and charging directly toward their goals. While they value hard work and determination, they also understand the importance of rest and self-care.

As the first earth sign of the zodiac, Taurus is a lover of earthly pleasures. No one appreciates good food, fresh air, and peaceful silence like a Taurus. They are especially grounded, with a firm understanding of themselves and their place in the world. Tauruses often struggle with change and push back against trying new things. If something worked for them in the past, why mess with it?

Tauruses make reliable lifelong friends, the kind who will help you fix a flat tire or remind you to take a vacation when you need it, but they may be hard to crack at first. They make caring and trustworthy partners, although they may show it more with their actions than their words. Tauruses prefer to work with their hands or have tangible results from their labor. Once they've found a job they like, they'll stick with it for the long haul.

Taurus Reading Life:

Tauruses read for pleasure, and they don't care what you think about their taste in books. They are likely to have a favorite genre and read only within that genre, rarely growing bored. Because they value honesty and lived experiences, they may prefer nonfiction, like history, biography, and, thanks to their love of gustatory delights, cookbooks. They don't get caught up in the world of buzzy new releases and enjoy rereading old favorites. Tauruses like long-term commitments, so you may find them reading a one-thousand-page book or an intimidatingly long series.

Since Tauruses read for their own enjoyment above all else, you're most likely to find them tucked away in the back corner of a library or reading alone in the park. You'll convince them to join a book club only if they already know and like everyone else in it. After all, who wants to talk about books when you could just be reading them? Their bookshelves are slimmed down to the essentials, holding only the books they already know and love.

Reading For Growth:

As Tauruses prefer to stick with what they know, they can learn from books that explore the positive aspects of change and trying something new. Books about trusting others and delegating may also be helpful, as Tauruses prefer tackling any task alone to

the uncertainty of handing it over to someone else. But let's be real: Tauruses don't like taking anyone's advice but their own.

Literary Soulmate: Cancer

Taurus and Cancer are naturally compatible as earth and water signs. When it comes to reading, they also share a tendency to read exclusively within their comfort genres. As long as they can agree on what that favorite genre is, they'll be happy as clams. And if not, both are perfectly content to read in companionable silence.

Famous Taurus Authors:

• Harper Lee—April 28: Like a classic Taurus, Lee didn't really care what others thought of her; she just wanted to do good work and enjoy a quiet, private life.

• Joy Harjo—May 9:

Harjo's determination and under-standing of the world around her led her to three terms as U.S. Poet Laureate, as well as making her a great teacher and activist.

Reading Recommendations

• The Broken Earth series by N.K. Jemisin

If you're looking for a long series to dig (heh) into, have we got one for you. The Broken Earth trilogy by N.K. Jemisin features a world in flux, as a massive geological event threatens the survival of humanity. But some of the world's inhabi-tants are already under threat: the orogenes, who have the power to manipulate the earth and have been shunned and controlled for those powers. This gritty, gets-under-your-fingernails story about some very determined char-acters is perfect for any Taurus, especially those who love science fiction and fantasy.

• *Northern Light* by Kazim Ali

There's nothing like beautiful writing and a compelling personal story, and *Northern Light* by Kazim Ali delivers both. Ali spent part of his immigrant childhood in a tiny outpost in Northern Canada; as an adult, he learns that the Native community there is facing an epi-demic of youth suicide. Revisiting the community means reconnect-ing to his own past and considering what it means to truly belong to one place, something he's never quite felt. Perfect for the Taurus thinking about roots versus root-lessness, or one who wants to learn about a unique place and people.

• *The Cheffe* by Marie NDiaye, translated by Jordan Stump
For the Taurus who loves a deep dive and all things food-related, *The Cheffe* is a must-read. This novel follows a famous, reclusive French chef for the full span of her life, all told from the perspective of one of her staff; but he's got his own agenda. *The Cheffe* delights the senses and the brain with its rich prose, descriptions of the chef's creations, and twists and turns as the narrative unfolds in unexpected directions. Make sure you've got snacks on hand, and maybe a notebook to jot down recipes you'll want to try!

• *Brave, Not Perfect: How Celebrating Imperfection Helps You Live Your Best, Most Joyful Life* by Reshma Saujani
Let's be real: Uncertainty is the worst, especially when you're a Taurus. But in *Brave, Not Perfect*, Reshma Saujani asks us to consider what life might look like if we let go of uncertainty and the fear of failure and were brave enough to try new things without guarantees that we'd be good at them. Not only does she talk about how this challenge shows up in her own life and in our society, but she breaks down specific techniques to add some courage and comfort with the unknown into your life. Give it a chance, and see where it takes you!

- *Spaceman of Bohemia* by Jaroslav Kalfař

Speaking of uncertainty: If there's any novel out there that asks you to let go of certainty (and the ground!) and embrace unknowingness, it's this one. Jakub Procházka is the Czech Republic's first astronaut, and when he's sent on a solo mission to investigate and sample an astronomical anomaly, things get . . . well, weird. Is he hallucinating or encountering alien life? Will he make it back to Earth? And what exactly has happened to his marriage? No answers here, only fascinating questions and lots of food for thought (and for a book club to argue about, if you're so inclined).

- *The Black Count* by Tom Reiss

You love a challenge, and you also love a classic. Tom Reiss covers both of those things in multiple ways in this fascinating dive into the history of the man behind *The Count of Monte Cristo* by Alexandre Dumas. In his quest to tell the story of General Alex Dumas, a forgotten figure and the inspiration for the classic, he travels to France to dig up records and then sends us back in time to the eighteenth century. You'll be swept away, learn a ton of "didja knows" to share with, well, everyone, and maybe even pick up *The Count*!

- *Wintering* by Katherine May
Tauruses love a goal, and a straight line toward that goal. But sometimes life just isn't like that. When May's own life got derailed, she used it as an opportunity to reacquaint herself with the comfort of rest and stillness—which you love as well! She pulls from classics of literature, science and the natural world, art, you name it, to think about what it means to pause and retreat (but not give up). Comforting as it confronts the hard times, *Wintering* is the perfect book for a Taurus looking for a reminder to stop and smell the roses.

Further Reading

- *Avatar, The Last Airbender: The Rise of Kyoshi* by F.C. Yee
- *Pilgrim at Tinker Creek* by Annie Dillard
- *Believers: Making a Life at the End of the World* by Lisa Wells

- *The Language of Baklava* by Diana Abu-Jaber
- *Trejo's Tacos: Recipes and Stories from L.A.* by Danny Trejo

Gemini

(May 21–June 20)

ELEMENT: Air
QUALITY: Mutable
RULING PLANET: Mercury
SYMBOL: The Twins

The Basics:

The quintessential devil's advocate, Geminis are masters of inhabiting different perspectives, which partially explains their symbol of "the twins." Geminis are often villainized as untrustworthy, gossipy, or flighty. But in reality, their curiosity and constant thirst for knowledge can be a good thing. Because of their wide array of interests, Geminis often have about fourteen different hobbies and side hustles at all times, usually seemingly unrelated.

In the life cycle of the zodiac, Gemini represents a curious toddler, always finding trouble in their exploration of the world. It's also the most charming sign of the zodiac; Geminis can start a conversation with just about anyone on any topic. And boy, do they love to talk! Their short attention spans also make them similar to toddlers; they're likely to wander off if the conversation grows stale.

Geminis are the best friends to bring as a plus-one to a social event, but they may flake on regularly scheduled plans. In romantic relationships, Geminis need someone full of surprises who can keep up with them intellectually, or else something shiny will draw them away. They prefer dynamic careers that let them constantly learn new skills and meet new people. Otherwise, they'll likely have many career changes throughout their lives or may balance multiple jobs at once.

Gemini Reading Life:

Geminis' insatiable curiosity makes them one of the biggest readers of the zodiac. They love reading across multiple genres, fiction and nonfiction, and rarely reread. Because of their short attention span, they often abandon books partway through or fail to finish a full series. They love books with multiple perspectives, retellings from the antagonist's point of view, and anything that makes them rethink their own perspective.

The twins also love the social aspects of the book world, enjoying every opportunity to discuss and debate the books they read. They can often be found at various book clubs, author events, and festivals. At home, their books are in disorganized stacks and chaotic bookshelves, threatening to eat them alive, but good luck convincing them to get rid of any.

Reading for Growth:

Because Geminis can have trouble sticking with something when it gets hard, they could learn from books about follow-through and seeing a project to its end. They're allergic to repetition, so books about the power of small routines and habits can be useful as well.

Literary Soulmate:
Scorpio

Gemini and Scorpio may not make a natural pairing, but when it comes to reading, they're a match made in library heaven. Both are fascinated by the workings of the human mind. They also both find likable characters to be overrated, much preferring the perspective of an intriguing villain.

Famous Gemini Authors:

• Akwaeke Emezi—June 6: Emezi's work showcases the twins' ability to play with binaries, perspective, and the idea of the self.

• Louise Erdrich—June 7: Beloved for her fiction, nonfiction, poetry, and children's books, as well as her independent bookstore, Erdrich is a classic Gemini jack-of-all-trades.

Reading Recommendations

• *Clap When You Land*
by Elizabeth Acevedo

This novel in verse told from two
sisters' perspectives is the perfect
match for the twins. The main
characters discover each other's
existence only after the death of
their father, which causes them to
reevaluate their lives, and gain-
ing new perspectives is one of
a Gemini's favorite things. The
poetic style and very different
settings will keep the attention of
the easily bored twins. The plot
also follows the tentative relationship that grows between these
sisters, which will charm this social
butterfly sign. This is also excellent
as an audiobook, which makes it a
great option for switching between
formats to keep it fresh.

• *Tiny Beautiful Things: Advice
on Love and Life from Dear
Sugar* by Cheryl Strayed

This is a collection of Cheryl
Strayed's "Dear Sugar" columns,
but don't be fooled: It is far from
saccharine. This is the perfect
book to get to see glimpses into
the most vulnerable moments of
strangers' lives, which is something
a nosy (I say that with love) Gemini
can't resist. Strayed answers questions from her column's readers
with compassion, kindness, and
painful realism. This will feed the
twins' desire to learn about other
people, while also containing
nuggets of advice that will remind
them to get their priorities straight

instead of flitting from existing projects to new opportunities without a backward glance.

• *Everfair* by Nisi Shawl
This is both a perfect Gemini read and a particular challenge for them. It's a steampunk alternate history of the Congo, told from every possible perspective: the existing king and queen of the region, Chinese workers brought in by the Belgian king, mixed-race European Everfair inhabitants, and more. The frequent perspective changes may test a Gemini's patience, but this epic that tackles colonialism, race, politics, war, espionage, grief, love, and betrayal is well worth it. This sign is always looking for a new angle on a subject, and this book offers almost every possible version of that, with complex characters and a decades-long scale.

• *The Checklist Manifesto: How to Get Things Right* by Atul Gawande
Geminis love starting a new project, but they don't always follow through. They're easily distracted by new possibilities and have trouble dealing with the details. This can lead to careless mistakes when they have to perform tasks they're not passionate about. *The Checklist Manifesto* is about adopting a simple habit—completing checklists—that has led to huge improvements in different fields, including saving lives during surgery. If the twins can sit still long enough to implement these changes, it could lead to big improvements in their professional and personal lives.

- *The Body Is Not an Apology: The Power of Radical Self-Love* by Sonya Renee Taylor

Geminis love befriending new people, and they often do this by adapting to the people around them. This can be healthy, but it's easy for the twins to lose touch with their authentic selves if they've been camouflaging too long—especially around people who are not accepting. *The Body Is Not an Apology* is a reminder for us to reclaim our bodies, including queer, POC, disabled, and other marginalized bodies. Geminis are often attracted to social issues, being so people-focused themselves, and this book provides a foundation to start fighting from by recognizing how different bodies are policed.

- *The Strange Case of Dr. Jekyll and Mr. Hyde* by Robert Louis Stevenson

Perhaps it's a cliché to recommend this classic two-faced character to the twins, but it's a good match even beyond that superficial reasoning. The duality of human nature is a fascinating subject for the ever-mercurial Gemini, and this is the perfect book to mull over those ideas. While this sign may shy away from reading classics in case they can't keep their (short) attention, *Dr. Jekyll and Mr. Hyde* is a slim book that packs a punch even if you already know the twist.

- *The Chosen and the Beautiful* by Nghi Vo

Whether or not you've read *The Great Gatsby*, this is a beautiful reimagining of the story that Geminis will love. Retellings and reimaginings attract this sign because they offer a window into how the same story changes when viewed from different perspectives, and Geminis want to be able to see them all. This is from the perspective of Jordan, a queer Vietnamese American who is both a part of and apart from the glitzy world she lives in. This retelling adds a touch of magic and ramps up the queer subtext of Nick and Gatsby to text.

Further Reading

- *Adaptation* by Malinda Lo
- *Falling in Love with Hominids* by Nalo Hopkinson
- *Strong Female Protagonist* by Brennan Lee Mulligan, illustrated by Molly Ostertag

- *The Summer We Got Free* by Mia McKenzie
- *The Truth About Stories: A Native Narrative* by Thomas King

Cancer

(June 21–July 22)

ELEMENT: Water

QUALITY: Cardinal

RULING PLANET: Moon

SYMBOL: The Crab

The Basics:

As the first water sign of the zodiac, Cancers recognize that emotions are valid and an integral part of being human. While earth and air signs think they can remove emotions from the equation, Cancers thrive on intuition and feelings, recognizing that all of our perceptions are tied to emotion. Like the crab that symbolizes them, Cancers can be a little hard to crack but will defend their loved ones fiercely. If you know a Cancer, you've probably seen them cry, and if you know one well, they've probably been there to support you when you've cried.

Cancers are creative, thoughtful, and caring. Family ties are incredibly important to them, and they highly value tradition and having a comfortable home. Because they wear their hearts on their sleeves, Cancers can be easily hurt and prone to mood swings, and can sometimes hold a grudge. But their connection to their own emotions means they are also very perceptive about the moods and feelings of others.

Although family always comes first, Cancers make devoted and caring friends. Look for a Cancer when you need to vent or want to cry over a sad movie with someone. Their emotional intelligence makes them wonderful romantic partners, if sometimes passive aggressive. Cancers do well in jobs that involve caring for others and working in teams, but can struggle to accept negative feedback.

Cancer Reading Life:

Cancers read for the emotional journey. They love books heavy on character development and internal struggle. The guaranteed happy ending of romance appeals to them, but they enjoy the angsty parts, too. In nonfiction, Cancers prefer personal stories like memoirs and autobiographies. The crab may return frequently to favorite childhood books or preferred comfort reads. They may forget details, but Cancers never forget how a book made them feel.

In the bookish world, you can find Cancers on bookstagram or review sites gushing about the books they love. Their ideal book club is one with a tight group of regulars who have stuck together for many years. At home, their bookshelves are a bit of a mess, but their reading nook is decked out with comfy pillows, warm blankets, and their favorite candle.

Reading for Growth:

Because Cancers tend to take things personally, books about growing a thicker skin, separating your home life from work, and learning to take constructive criticism may be useful. Lessons on letting things go and moving on from loss could also curb their habit of holding a grudge.

Literary Soulmate:
Taurus

Cancer and Taurus are naturally compatible as water and earth signs. When it comes to reading, they also share a tendency to read exclusively within their comfort genres. As long as they can agree on what that favorite genre is, they'll be happy as clams. And if not, both are perfectly content to read in companionable silence.

Famous Cancer Authors:

• Octavia E. Butler—June 22: The nuanced understanding of humanity and emotional intelligence of Butler's work, a Cancer signature, made her one of the most iconic science fiction authors of all time.

• Jhumpa Lahiri—July 11: Lahiri's writing on family ties, generational memory, and personal growth over time is about as Cancer as it gets.

Reading Recommendations

- *Girl Woman Other*
by Bernardine Evaristo
Emotional journey? Check.
Character development? Check.
Internal struggle? Check! This
incredible novel, told in prose-
poem form, will suck you right in
and carry you along on a journey
that explores what it means to be
a person—often female, often
Black—in the U.K. Each character
gets a moment in the sun to share
their story, and each is struggling
to find their way through their
own unique obstacles and traumas.
You'll feel all the feelings along
with them, so come prepared with
tissues; there's a reason this book
won the Booker Prize!

- *The Switch* by Beth O'Leary
Maybe you want the feelings but
less on the heavy side and more
on the fun side, with a guaranteed
happy ending—in which case what
you want is *The Switch*. Leena is
in her late twenties, burnt-out at
work, and struggling with grief;
her grandmother Eileen is newly
single at seventy-nine and ready
for an adventure. So, naturally, they
swap! Leena takes up residence
in Eileen's cozy cottage in a small
town, while Eileen moves into
Leena's city apartment and starts
living it up. A chef's-kiss of a feel-
good story, complete with laughs.

- *Spirit Run: A 6,000-Mile Marathon Through North America's Stolen Land* by Noé Álvarez

What does one do when the feelings get to be too much? Well, Noé Álvarez left college and embarked on a four-month-long marathon across the Americas, to honor the Native populations and reconnect with his own Mexican heritage. His journey is both geographic and personal, complete with guides and literal and metaphorical roadblocks. This memoir honors his own and his fellow runners' struggles to locate their identities within the diaspora of North America and allows you to run alongside them every step of the way. Whether you're an armchair traveler or a seasoned one, this is a journey you'll want to share.

- *When Things Fall Apart: Heart Advice for Difficult Times* by Pema Chödrön

When you're as in touch with your feelings as a Cancer can be, it's hard to move on from painful situations. Chödrön, whose life advice is always kindly and compassionately delivered, is here to help you sort out how. Whether it's using those difficult emotions to grow, figuring out how to move on from the harm someone else has done you, or sorting out how to talk with others about that harm, she offers thoughtful, practical advice and strategies. Whatever your spiritual practices (or lack thereof), there's something here for you.

• *The Magical Language of Others* by E.J. Koh

If there ever was a memoir about letting go of a grudge, it's this one. Koh was deeply scarred when, during her teen years, her mother moved with her father back to South Korea so he could take a high-paying job, leaving Koh with her older brother in California. The experience forever changed her life; how do you forgive something like that? As she works on translating the letters her mother sent her over the years, Koh contemplates just that. This stunning memoir digs into family grief and trauma and helps remind us that everyone has their own story.

• *The Ones We're Meant to Find* by Joan He

This sister story in a potentially not-so-distant future will sweep you away on two journeys: one, in a futurist city in the clouds in which Kasey is trying to find her missing sister; and one on a deserted island, as Cee tries to figure out where all the people are. As these stories twine around each other, it's an opportunity for us to not only be along for the ride but consider what it means to be human, to be a good citizen, and above all, what we will (or won't) do for family. A veritable food-for-thought cornucopia for Cancers!

• *Honey Girl* by Morgan Rogers Calling all water signs: This book is not only full of flowing language and oceanic metaphors, it's also the perfect story for people who need to learn to let go of all the expectations and fears of their own and of others. As Grace Porter tries to figure out what comes next after hitting all her key milestones, a new relationship helps shed light on some old, worn-out personal baggage. This book is a celebration of the struggles and joys of finding your path, a comfort read, and a self-care manual all in one.

Further Reading

• *Howl's Moving Castle* by Diana Wynne Jones

• *The Prey of Gods* by Nicky Drayden
• *Thanks for Waiting: The Joy (& Weirdness) of Being a Late Bloomer* by Doree Shafrir
• *The Night Watchman* by Louise Erdrich
• *The Pretty One: On Life, Pop Culture, Disability, and Other Reasons to Fall in Love with Me* by Keah Brown

Leo

(July 23–August 22)

———•———•———•———

ELEMENT: Fire
QUALITY: Fixed
RULING PLANET: Sun
SYMBOL: The Lion

The Basics:

Leo, represented by the lion, is indeed the king of the jungle. Charismatic, confident, and driven, Leos are the classic fairytale heroes of the zodiac. As a fire sign, they also have a healthy ego and sense of competition. If you ask a Leo, they'll tell you that they're the best sign, but that may also be because it's the only sign they've bothered to learn anything about.

Their passion and skills of persuasion make Leos great leaders, and they have a special talent for uniting people behind a common cause. They live by the motto "Work hard, play hard," loving the spotlight both at the office and during their leisure time. However, all of the attention and praise they tend to receive can go to their heads, making them a bit self-centered and vain at their worst. But even during an ego trip, it's hard to hold a grudge against the mighty lion.

As friends, Leos love giving a good pep talk and reminding you of your best qualities, but they see you as a supporting character and themselves as the star. In love, Leos will protect you fiercely and love you (almost) as much as themselves. Leos make natural managers and leaders; however, they'll quickly grow frustrated with a job if they feel undervalued.

Leo Reading Life:

Leos enjoy books where they can picture themselves in the shoes of the hero, so they love a strong protagonist. Fantasy, superhero, and crime-solving narratives are particular favorites, especially when they can follow a beloved character through a series. As they care a lot about appearances, they may sometimes choose books based on what they think other people will find impressive.

Since they love seeing their favorite characters brought to life,

Leos are first in line for buzzy film adaptations of books. They also appreciate a book club where they can lead the conversation and dazzle others with their insights. Their bookshelves are carefully organized to showcase the books they most want visitors to know they read.

Reading for Growth:

Because Leos can be a bit self-absorbed, books about empathy and appreciating other perspectives could be useful. They make great leaders but can also be a little intense, so Leos could learn from books about thoughtful and sensitive management.

Literary Soulmate:
Aquarius

Leo's fire and Aquarius's air elements make them a fairly compatible pairing. When it comes to books, they've both got a soft spot for a plucky protagonist fighting to save the world. They can agree on fantasy, sci-fi, comics, memoir, and history books, particularly ones with badass heroes.

Famous Leo Authors:

• James Baldwin—August 2: Leo's passion and drive are showcased in Baldwin's unforgettable work, as well as in his leadership in the civil rights movement.

• Suzanne Collins—August 10: Collins's massively popular Hunger Games series shows she's a Leo who has truly mastered the art of the hero.

Reading Recommendations

• *Shuri: The Search for Black Panther* by Nnedi Okorafor (writer) and Leonardo Romero (artist)

Leos in search of a strong hero and a popular character from a buzzy franchise should get to know techno genius Shuri. In this volume of the Shuri comics, the Black Panther's sister shows she's not afraid to step up and lead Wakanda when T'Challa disappears while on a mission in space. Shuri embodies the role of the lioness with a mind for strategy, fierce determination, and the strength and heart needed to protect her pride. Not only will Leos relish Shuri's center-stage moment, they'll have reason to flex their extroversion by sharing their fandom with other Black Panther fans wherever they meet them.

- *The Queen of the Night* by Alexander Chee
Give Leos the spotlight and this sweeping historical fiction follow-ing Lilliet Berne from America to Second Empire France, from rags to riches, from unknown status to celebrity. Born an orphan, Lilliet is the star of the Paris Opera and lives up to her fame with a knack for glamour and a rare, uncanny voice. But life isn't all champagne

and salons for our natural-born star. When an original role lands on Lilliet's doorstep, promising her an opportunity to be immortalized, she recognizes in it something far less savory: an exposé revealing her deepest, most closely kept secret. Prima donnas, get ready for a page-turner.

- *The Rib King* by Ladee Hubbard
Shake your mane and call yourself iconic. Given the chance, Leos might sign on the dotted line to become the face of a brand. But what's the cost? In this buzzy and insightful historical fiction with a mystery twist about African American stereotypes and their victims, we're introduced to an early twentieth-century upstairs-downstairs tale about the Black servants of a wealthy white house-hold. When the Barclays strike up a deal to exploit their Black cook's rib sauce and loyal groundskeeper

August Sitwell gets caricatured on the bottle, Sitwell's newfound fame becomes a double-edged sword while maid Jennie Williams sets off to find her own, self-made status as a household name.

• *Klara and the Sun* by Kazuo Ishiguro

an AF—an artificial friend—ready to do her best as a companion to young Josie. In this domestic science fiction novel, Klara watches as Josie faces both familiar and unfamiliar coming-of-age challenges—changing relationships, peer pressure, and the complexities of being "elevated," to name a few. Klara and her story will take Leos on an introspective journey, challenging them to see the world through the eyes of someone who is focused on others, and whose love is quiet, but deep.

Have you ever aspired to be the fly on the wall? To observe from the sidelines, at peace with your role as the shadow? Thought not, Leo. See the world from the other side—Klara's side. Klara is

- *The Power of Vulnerability: Teachings on Authenticity, Connection, and Courage* by Brené Brown

Leo, we know you're brave and hungry to share your best qualities with the world, but let's take a minute to consider vulnerability and what it can teach us. Research professor and expert Brené Brown is here to dispel myths about vulnerability as a weakness, to promote the benefits of dropping that armor, and to offer new ways to define and engender courage. Leos feel powerful as they are, but this personal development book provides a toolkit that might be missing from their repertoire. Who needs bluster and peacocking when you can shed that flashy getup and show people who you really are?

- *Anne of Green Gables* by Lucy Maud Montgomery

Here comes a heroine to follow through a strong series of books, and then to revisit again and again. In Lucy Maud Montgomery's widely read classic, strong-willed and imaginative Anne Shirley shines fierce and bright as the summer sun from the moment she steps out of the orphanage and into the lives of Marilla and Matthew Cuthbert at Green Gables. Anne's irrepressible flair for the dramatic, intense loyalty, and undying love for her nearest and dearest will resonate with Leos. As with the fiery felines of the zodiac, Anne is hard to dislike even at her worst—she might have gotten you drunk on currant wine, but she'll always have your back.

• *Mem* by Bethany Morrow

While Leos are drawn to larger-than-life characters, they would benefit from the perspective of a hero relegated to the sidelines and shadowy spaces. A character kept in a vault, left there to be forgotten and live a seemingly mindless, circular life. While Dolores Extract #1 was created to be anything but the main character even of her own life, her penchant for quiet observation makes her something miraculous. She is an extracted memory capable of creating her own memories, rather than endlessly living out the traumas of the person from whom she was cloned. Dolores is not only a scientific marvel but also a source of empathy and a unique model of leadership Leos could stand to learn from.

Further Reading

• *Not Your Sidekick* by C.B. Lee
• *Nothing to See Here* by Kevin

Wilson
• *Quiet: The Power of Introverts in a World That Can't Stop Talking* by Susan Cain
• *These Ghosts Are Family* by Maisy Card
• *Uprooted* by Naomi Novik

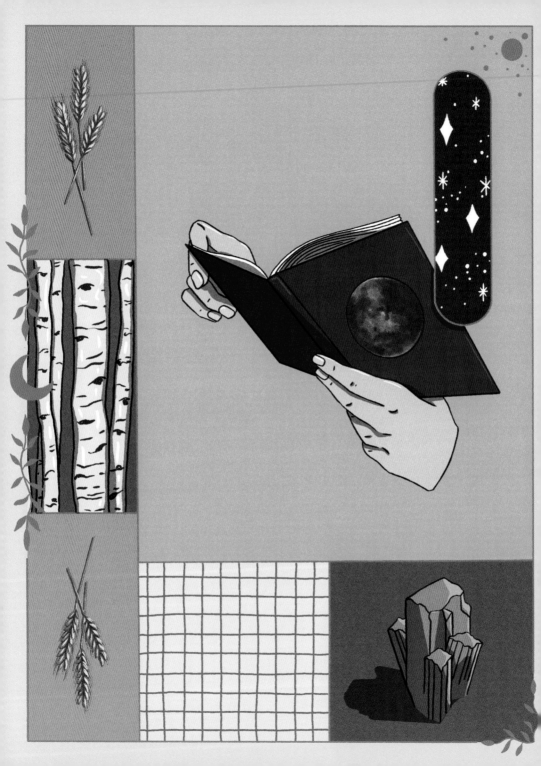

Virgo

(August 23–September 22)

ELEMENT: Earth
QUALITY: Mutable
RULING PLANET: Mercury
SYMBOL: The Maiden

The Basics:

If you want something done right, ask a Virgo. Their methodical approach to life, attention to detail, and signature earth sign practicality make Virgos some of the hardest workers of the zodiac. Virgo is symbolized by the maiden, said to be based on the Greek goddess Astraea, the last immortal figure to abandon Earth for Olympus. Similarly, Virgos have great hope for humanity, but often find themselves disappointed when others fall short of their expectations. Virgos' expectations are always the highest for themselves, and they're the hardest on themselves, too. Picture Virgos like swimming ducks: cool, calm, and collected on the surface, but paddling furiously under the water.

Every single Virgo has "detail-oriented" on their résumé, or at least they should. They are organizational and project management masterminds, but all of that time spent analyzing the minutiae can mean they sometimes struggle to see the forest for the trees. They value facts above emotions and guard their hearts fiercely.

Virgos prefer a small number of close friends to large social groups, and they're often the "mom friend" who ensures you pack a sweater and won't let you forget a meal. In relationships, they have very high, nonnegotiable standards, but if you pass muster, they're dedicated and affectionate. They prefer jobs with clear expectations and little gray area, and they expect nothing but perfect performance from themselves and anyone they manage.

Virgo Reading Life:

Because life as a Virgo can be pretty stressful, they love reading for relaxation. But because of their attention to detail, nothing pulls them out of a good story faster than plot holes, small inconsistencies, and typos. Virgos love fantasy with carefully constructed worlds and murder mysteries that drop just the right amount of hints for them to guess whodunnit. In nonfiction, they love a carefully constructed argument with concrete evidence.

Nothing brings the bookish Virgo more joy than a well-organized library or bookstore, although they may have some ideas on how to arrange it just a little bit better. Their bookshelves at home have a very intense system of order, and they will absolutely notice if you move something. Virgos who bookstagram can spend hours trying to get the perfectly balanced shot—often longer than they actually spent reading the book.

Reading for Growth:

Virgos tend to get caught up in the details, so books about seeing the big picture and the value of "good enough" can be useful. Reading about trusting others and going easier on yourself may also be productive for the Virgo with unreasonable standards for themselves and the people around them.

Literary Soulmate: Sagittarius

Virgo and Sagittarius both have a "my way or the highway" attitude that could cause them to clash. But when it comes to reading, they might just find they're on the same highway. Both like to see comprehensive, thoughtful world building and a chance to escape the mundane through thrilling books. They can also bond over their shared pet peeve of typos, plot holes, and inconsistencies they can't let go.

Famous Virgo Authors:

- N.K. Jemisin—September 19: Jemisin is a classic Virgo perfectionist, whose detailed world building and ability to carry out a series have made her a legend in science fiction and fantasy writing.

• George R.R. Martin—
September 20:
Perhaps the reason Martin has yet to finish the Game of Thrones series is because he's holding his writing to impossibly high Virgo standards.

Reading Recommendations

• *Everything I Never Told You* by Celeste Ng
Because Virgos have high standards for their reading, this carefully crafted narrative should be a perfect match. There is a mystery element—the teenage daughter is dead at the beginning of the book, and everyone is trying to understand how it happened—but it's also a portrait of a family told from each member's perspective. We see the things they are hiding from each other, the subtle indignities and resentments.

Virgo readers will appreciate Ng's skillful language and her nuanced exploration of how racism and sexism affect this family in small and fundamental ways.

• *Fingersmith* by Sarah Waters
The detail-oriented Virgo will appreciate the many twists and turns this book takes, connecting characters and plot points in unexpected ways. Sue is a "fingersmith" (a thief) who is brought into a scheme to pose as a maid for a wealthy woman in order to con her out of her fortune. Sue will convince Maude to marry Gentleman, he will have her institutionalized, and Sue and Gentleman will split the money. There's only one problem: Sue has fallen in love with Maude. This is an intricate, stunning book that rewards the careful attention that a Virgo reader will bring to it.

• *Why Fish Don't Exist: A Story of Loss, Love, and the Hidden Order of Life* by Lulu Miller
Ostensibly, this is a biography of David Starr Jordan, a taxonomist of fish. The reason Lulu Miller is retelling his life story, though, is because she turned to it as a source of inspiration in a chaotic, meaningless world. Her deep dive into this fairly obscure scientific figure unearths a compelling story that demonstrates how the detail-oriented focus that Virgos excel at can be so fruitful. This is a narrative that skillfully winds together a biography of Jordan, a memoir of Miller's search for meaning, and fascinating scientific facts and anecdotes.

• *The Pursuit of Perfect: How to Stop Chasing and Start Living a Richer, Happier Life* by Tal Ben-Shahar
Perfectionism is an almost inescapable Virgo trait, which is why it's worthwhile for this sign to reconsider whether these high standards are helping or hindering them. Ben-Shahar uses scientific principles of positive psychology—principles he's been teaching in his popular Harvard course for years—to determine what actually makes people happier in life. The answer? Failure can teach us lessons, and true fulfilment doesn't come from being perfect. The author makes a distinction between negative perfectionism and positive perfectionism, or "optimalism." *The Pursuit of Perfect* will help Virgos learn how to harness their perfectionism for greater life satisfaction.

• *See No Stranger: A Memoir and Manifesto of Revolutionary Love* by Valerie Kaur

The Virgo's high standards for themselves and others can lead to resentment and anger when other people don't live up to them. *See No Stranger* is an invitation to love others—and yourself—from a revolutionary, compassionate, and curious place. Kaur does not shy away from the difficulties of loving your opponents or people you fundamentally disagree with: She describes growing up as the target of xenophobia and racism, especially in the aftermath of 9/11.

This book describes love for the world not as passive acceptance but as part of a revolutionary framework, which will appeal to the justice-minded Virgo.

• The Lord of the Rings trilogy by J. R. R. Tolkien
While some other signs might chafe at Tolkien's long, loving descriptions of scenery, Virgos will appreciate the careful world building and depth in this epic fantasy. This is a series that is all about the details, and it will reward the close reading that Virgos can't help but bring to their pleasure reading. Expect this sign to also pick up *The Silmarillion* to make sure they haven't missed any minutiae of Middle Earth, from its languages and culture to its landscape and history. While many readers have read and loved LOTR, Virgos will immerse themselves in it.

- *Rest: Why You Get More Done When You Work Less* by Alex Soojung-Kim Pang

A Virgo's high standards can lead to stress and even burnout when nothing feels like enough. Their inability to bring anything less than their best to their job can manifest in workaholism. *Rest* is uniquely suited to Virgos because it not only extols the joys of doing nothing but also argues that building in self-care and deliberate rest will in fact make us more productive, creative, and successful. While resting for the sake of it might be a tough pill to swallow for this sign, recognizing that it's an essential part of a successful life is a framing that has a better chance of getting through.

Further Reading

- *A Wizard of Earthsea* by Ursula K. Le Guin
- *Butter Honey Pig Bread* by Francesca Ekwuyasi
- *Stamped from the Beginning: The Definitive History of Racist Ideas in America* by Ibram X. Kendi
- *The Argonauts* by Maggie Nelson
- *The Hidden Keys* by André Alexis

Libra

(September 23–October 22)

ELEMENT: Air

QUALITY: Cardinal

RULING PLANET: Venus

SYMBOL: The Scales

The Basics:

Everyone loves a Libra. You know why? Because Libras work really damn hard to make everyone happy. That's partially because they highly value peace, harmony, and equality. It's also partially because they just love good vibes. Libra is symbolized by the scales, highlighting their love of balance and fairness in all things. That desire to make others happy means that a Libra is also likely to put their own needs last. In the life cycle of the zodiac, Libra represents a new adult, trying to find their place in the world and often too concerned about others' perceptions of them.

Libras care deeply about the space around them and creating an atmosphere that looks, sounds, smells, tastes, and feels pleasant. They spend a lot of time decorating their space, making the perfect playlist, and picking just the right essential oils for their mood. Some may interpret this as an obsession with material things, but for Libras, it's all about how your setting affects the mind. They host excellent parties, and their communication skills make them great mediators.

Libras have tons of friends from all walks of life, although their tendency to tell friends what they want to hear makes them a bit hard to really know. In love, Libras go above and beyond to make their partners happy, sometimes holding on to relationships that aren't serving them. When it comes to work, Libras do well in fields that require strong communication and interpersonal skills, and they respond well to frequent praise.

Libra Reading Life:

Thanks to their love of balance, Libras enjoy reading across a variety of genres. They often read multiple books at a time so they can pick up whichever one best suits their mood. Atmospheric books like descriptive historical fiction, noir, or horror are particular favorites, since they read for the vibes. In nonfiction, they like memoirs and biographies of people trying to make the world a more peaceful place.

Bookshelves are an opportunity for Libras to create the perfect aesthetic, so they love a rainbow bookshelf and decorating their reading nook with lots of plants. They love the feel of being in a bookstore, particularly one with a good café, but their indecisiveness can lead them to spend hours trying to decide exactly what to buy. In book clubs, they avoid conflict and focus instead on finding the perfect next book that the whole group will love.

Reading for Growth:

Because Libras tend to put others before themselves, books about self-care and prioritizing your own

needs are a must. Libras may also enjoy learning more about decorating, gardening, cooking, and other things that make their home lives cozier.

Literary Soulmate:
Pisces

Libra and Pisces both have a tendency to put others before themselves, although they may go about it in different ways. When it comes to books, they can bond over their love of feel-good books and atmospheric writing that gives them all the right vibes. They also share a passion for creating the perfect comfy reading spot.

Famous Libra Authors:

- R.L. Stine—October 8: Talk about a vibe! Stine's Goosebumps series shows that he has mastered the art of the atmospheric novel.

- Marie Kondo—October 9: Kondo has made a career out of helping people improve their surroundings, and no one but a Libra could come up with the idea of keeping only things that "spark joy."

Reading Recommendations

- *Mexican Gothic* by Silvia Moreno-Garcia

Gather round, Libras, for all the twisty, unsettling, horror vibes of your dreams (nightmares?). Fashionable Mexico City socialite Noemí receives a cryptic letter from her newly wed cousin Catalina that reads like a cry for help. Noemí heads to High Place, the creepy ol' house in the mountains of Hidalgo where her cousin lives, and Catalina's English husband, Virgil, insists that tuberculosis made Catalina write the nonsensical letter. Noemí isn't buying that noise, though, and what begins as a slow, simmering uneasiness boils into full-blown disturbia as Noemí discovers the secrets hidden in High Place. Reader, I apologize in advance about the mushrooms.

- *A Master of Djinn* by P. Djèlí Clark

This is the first full-length novel in the Dead Djinn universe, a fantastic series set in 1912 in an alternative, magical, steampunk Cairo. Special Investigator Fatma el-Sha'arawi, the youngest woman at the Ministry of Alchemy, Enchantments, and Supernatural Entities, is investigating the killing of a brotherhood dedicated to al-Jahiz, the famed Sudanese mystic who tore a hole in the veil between the magical and mundane worlds before disappearing. The man claiming responsibility for the killings claims to be al-Jahiz returned, but how can that be? Together with the partner she isn't sure she wants and her lover, Fatma sets out to uncover the truth about this self-professed prophet. Libra readers will come for the immersive world building and noir detective vibes and stay for the queer feminist heroine kicking ass and taking names. Oh, and let's not forget the searing indictment of colonialism and all it brings with it.

• *The Compton Cowboys: The New Generation of Cowboys in America's Urban Heartland* by Walter Thompson-Hernández

Hey, Libra: You look like you could use a hopeful read about folks trying to cultivate hope and healing in the world. Allow me to introduce you to the Compton Cowboys, a group of ten Black riders on a small ranch in Compton, California, the last in an area that's been home to African American horse riders for decades. It all started with the Compton Jr. Posse, a project founded by Mayisha Akbar in 1988 to offer local youth an alternative to street life. Today the Cowboys are a group of Black men and women defying stereotypes in a community built on camaraderie, healing, and recovery.

• *Hana Khan Carries On* by Uzma Jalaluddin
When Hana Khan isn't working at her parents' restaurant, the only halal restaurant in their Toronto neighborhood, she's interning at a radio station with dreams of telling stories of her own. When plans are announced for a new upscale halal place to open in the 'hood, Hana decides to sabotage the

opening before it threatens her family's business—if her growing attraction to the rival restaurant's owner doesn't get in the way first. Hana spends so much time trying to do for others that she forgets about her own hopes and dreams, a sacrifice no one really asked her to make. Let this be a sign to put yourself first, Libra. You can't take care of others if you don't first take care of yourself.

- *Over the Top: A Raw Journey to Self-Love* by Jonathan Van Ness

Today, *Queer Eye* grooming and self-care expert Jonathan Van Ness is a joyful beacon of light, positivity, and back handsprings for the 'gram, but getting to that healthy outlook was a journey. This raw and heartfelt memoir takes readers back through Van Ness's childhood in a midwestern town that found him too bold, too gay,

too much. The journey to self-love isn't always an easy one, Libra.

- *Practical Magic* by Alice Hoffman

Libras love a mood read and so I present to you the vibes: witchy vibes, sister vibes, small New England town vibes, all the vibes! This witchy classic is the first book in what decades later would become a series of four books about the inimitable Owens women. In *Practical Magic*, we first meet Sally and Gillian and their eccentric aunts Franny and Jet, four women descended from one powerful witch who cursed the women in her family to keep them from falling in love. The books are a celebration of sisterhood, of women, and of big, sweeping, can't-live-without-you love.

- *Hill House Living: The Art of Creating a Joyful Life* by Paula Sutton

You crave cozy perfection: a space that perfectly blends form and function with thoughtful touches and comfortable delights. Allow me then to introduce you to Paula Sutton, the delightful English influencer known by thousands as @hillhousevintage on the 'gram. You may not have the perfect little cottage in the English countryside like she does, but you can still soak up all that Sutton has to share on antiques hunting, gardening, and enjoying the seasons. Get ready to reach maximum cozy and chic.

Further Reading

- *Everything's Trash, but It's Okay* by Phoebe Robinson
- *Night Theater* by Vikram Paralkar
- *Survival of the Thickest* by Michelle Buteau

- *The Forest of Stolen Girls* by June Hur
- *The Only Good Indians* by Stephen Graham Jones

Scorpio

(October 23–November 21)

ELEMENT: Water

QUALITY: Fixed

RULING PLANETS: Pluto and Mars

SYMBOL: The Scorpion

The Basics:

Scorpios are perhaps the most villainized sign of the zodiac. They can keep a calm, unreadable exterior while secretly carrying out their decades-long plot for power, making them the ideal comic book super villain. But if you've stayed on the good side of a Scorpio, you know that they have the caring, emotional, marshmallow center of a water sign deep down under their carefully protected exterior. Much like the scorpion that symbolizes them, people tend to forget Scorpio's other cool features once they've suffered their venomous sting.

Incredibly passionate and determined, nothing can stop a Scorpio once they've set their mind on a goal. Due to their hatred of dishonesty and tendency to take themselves very seriously, Scorpios can easily feel betrayed and seek revenge that seems disproportionate. But if you prove yourself trustworthy, Scorpios are incredibly loyal and protective of their inner circle. Scorpios tend to have strong relationships with their family, although they're not afraid to cut a relative off if the relationship is no longer serving them.

Scorpios can be one of the hardest signs to get to know, but once you've passed their test, they'll never leave your side. That is, unless you piss them off. In love, Scorpios are mysterious, magnetic, and passionate, but they will ruin your life if you ever break up with them. Their passion and determination make them great leaders, and Scorpios thrive in careers that give them some level of power.

Scorpio Reading Life:

Scorpio's analytical mind and emotional water-sign base make them perhaps the most intuitive when it comes to human nature. For that reason, they love reading about complex, imperfect protagonists, and they especially appreciate a well-crafted villain. Character-driven narratives tend to draw their attention more than an action-packed plot. Psychological thrillers, heists, and revenge narratives are particular favorites. When it comes to nonfiction, they enjoy true crime and memoirs by unapologetically powerful people.

In the bookish world, you can find Scorpios fiercely defending their favorite authors at book clubs and on social media and giving one-star reviews on every platform to books written by authors who've upset them. Scorpios' bookshelves in more visible parts of their homes are carefully curated to not give anything away about their personal lives. But somewhere deep in a hidden closet is their secret book-shelf of feel-good fiction, along with their squishy, comfortable, private reading nook.

Reading for Growth:

Because Scorpios can hold an intense grudge, they can learn from reading about forgiveness and empathy. They could also use a lesson in enjoying the journey of life more than the destination. But let's be real: You're more likely to find a Scorpio reading self-help books on war tactics and using manipulation to get what they want.

Literary Soulmate:
Gemini

Scorpio and Gemini may not make a natural pairing, but when it comes to reading, they're a match made in library heaven. Both are fascinated by the workings of the human mind. They also find likable characters to be overrated, much preferring the perspective of an intriguing villain.

Famous Scorpio Authors:

- Colson Whitehead—
November 6:
Perhaps Scorpio's passion and drive have helped Whitehead win an incredible list of awards, from the Pulitzer Prize for Fiction to a MacArthur genius grant.

- Margaret Atwood—
November 18:
Atwood's writing is a perfect example of Scorpio's deep under-standing of human nature's flaws, as well as the power politics that shape society.

Reading Recommendations

- *Our Kind of Cruelty*
by Araminta Hall
This book has big Scorpio energy from the deeply flawed and unreli-able narrator to the twisty ending, not to mention the psychological mind game of trying to figure out what is what. Mike Hayes's childhood was dark and lonely, but that was before he met Verity Metcalf. It's because of V that Mike learned how to love, how to care for himself, how to get his career in order. Yep, Verity is the love of his life, and together they'll build something beautiful and ride off into the sunset! I mean sure, she's not returning his calls, and she's technically engaged to someone else. It'll all just be part of a secret game they play. Right?

- *The Gilded Wolves*
by Roshani Chokshi
We on Team Scorpio love a good heist novel and this lush, glam-orous historical YA fantasy does not disappoint. Treasure hunter and wealthy hotelier Séverin Montagnet-Alarie is your guy if you're looking for the skinny on secrets in Belle Époque Paris. When an all-powerful society called the Order of Babel seeks him out for a job, he's offered a treasure he just can't refuse: his

true inheritance. He gathers up a merry band of magical misfits to get the job done, and they go in with a plan, of course. But you know what they say about plans . . . the Scorpios among us delighted in all the secrets and treachery, plus a villain whom you'll kind of love to hate.

• *Women and Other Monsters: Building a New Mythology* by Jess Zimmerman

Unapologetic power plus complex characters is one Scorpio-tastic combo, and this book delivers with a delicious side of feminism. This cultural analysis of female monsters from Greek mythology dedicates one chapter to each of eleven monstrous women, including Medusa, the Harpies, the Furies, Scylla, and the Sphinx. The author asks readers to examine depictions of women's hunger, anger, ugliness, and ambition in literature, traits that are so often vilified in women but explained away or extolled in men. She challenges women to reclaim the monster label because monsters get a certain kind of freedom that "well-behaved" women rarely do: the freedom to be messy, to be larger than life.

• *Once Upon a Quinceañera* by Monica Gomez-Hira Carmen Aguilar is retaking an internship class that means working as a Dream, a dancing, singing Disney princess at kid parties. It's kind of fun until the Dreams are hired to perform at the quinceañera of the cousin who ruined Carmen's reputation, and the ex who broke her heart just joined the Dream team, too (rude!). Her high school diploma is riding on this internship, so she'll have to find a way to get along with her ex and stop her spoiled prima from ruining her own quinceañera. Carmen is prickly and angry AF for so much of the book, but she learns the healing power of forgiveness in time—a valuable lesson for the grudge-holding Scorpio.

• *Notes from a Young Black Chef* by Kwame Onwuachi with Joshua David Stein

By age twenty-seven, former *Top Chef* contestant Kwame Onwuachi had both opened and closed Shaw Bijou, one of the buzziest fine-dining establishments in America. The restaurant was the embodiment of his entire culinary vision, from the flavors on his menu to the lighting fixtures and the diversity of his kitchen staff. To understand why it failed—and why, more importantly, it didn't mean the end of his career—Onwuachi takes us back to his beginnings. The Scorpio who could use a lesson in seeing the forest for the trees will find a lot that resonates in this memoir about finding your place in the world, falling on your face a few times, and still enjoying the ride.

• *The Count of Monte Cristo* by Alexandre Dumas

You relish a good revenge story and this here is a classic. After he's wrongly—but deliberately—imprisoned for a crime he did not commit, Edmond Dantes learns of a treasure hoard that's said to be hidden on the Isle of Monte Cristo. He decides he's going to escape from prison, find that treasure, and unleash some vengeful fury on the people responsible for his imprisonment. Sure, this book is about love, faith, and redemption. But Scorpio, let's be real: Alexandre Dumas's meaty tome is dripping with cold, meticulously plotted, hard-won revenge. Delicious.

• *The Road Trip* by Beth O'Leary Addie and Dylan once spent the summer falling in love under the Provence sun. But their wild, romantic, sun-drenched affair is now a thing of the past, making it real inconvenient when Dylan rear-ends Addie on the way to a mutual friend's wedding. With no other options available, they decide to put the past behind them for the weekend and car-pool together. . . . What could go wrong?! The cast of secondary characters and chaotic ride to this wedding in rural Scotland will do you good, Scorpio: The laughs will keep you turning the page, and the unfolding of Addie and Dylan's story is a much-needed reminder that it's more about the journey than the destination.

Further Reading

• *A Tip for the Hangman* by Allison Epstein
• *My Sister, the Serial Killer* by Oyinkan Braithwaite
• *The Five: The Untold Lives of the Women Killed by Jack the Ripper* by Hallie Rubenhold
• *The Wild Woman's Guide to Traveling the World* by Kristin Rockaway

Sagittarius
(November 22–December 21)

ELEMENT: Fire
QUALITY: Mutable
RULING PLANET: Jupiter
SYMBOL: The Archer

The Basics:

Love them or hate them, you can trust a Sagittarius to never be anything but their truest selves. In the life cycle of the zodiac, Sagittarius is firmly middle-aged and has learned a lot about the world around them and their place in it. Represented by the archer, Sagittarius is known for always being a straight shooter. They highly value honesty and don't believe in coddling while dropping hard truths.

The biggest traveler of the zodiac, Sagittarius loves to explore other landscapes, cultures, and histories. They especially love venturing off the beaten path. Anything too mundane or "normal" will quickly bore the archer. Sagittarius is never afraid of being alone, always preferring their own company to that of someone who might annoy them. And believe me, they'll have no problem telling you if you rub them the wrong way.

As a friend, a Sagittarius is the perfect person to have by your side while trying something out of the ordinary or to give you real talk when you need it. But don't count on a Sagittarius if you need someone to be gentle with your feelings. In relationships, a Sagittarius needs someone who can match them intellectually and has their own unique set of interests. They'd rather be single than be in a boring relationship. At work, the archer prefers jobs that let them travel and take big risks, and they have little tolerance for meetings that should have been emails.

Sagittarius Reading Life:

Sagittarius's yearning for fresh perspectives and new experiences makes them prolific readers. They'll read anything, as long as it gives them something new to consider and isn't too predictable. Their love of travel draws them to books set in unique locations or historical fiction that helps them travel to another time. As the straight-shooting archer, they also prefer nonfiction that focuses on the facts to flowery prose.

In the bookish world, you can find Sagittarians gleefully starting fights at book clubs and ruining your favorite book by pointing out plot holes. They love roaming a library or bookstore and choosing a random book based on the cover. At home, Sagittarius has books stacked on every available surface, and they've actually read most of them. It's unclear why they hold on to so many of them, as Sagittarians rarely reread.

Reading for Growth:

Patience is a struggle for Sagittarians, so books about taking things slow and appreciating the simple things could be helpful. As they're likely to quickly pass judgment and ignore evidence that proves them wrong, they may also

benefit from books about keeping an open mind. And since they're fans of adventure, any tips for travelers could come in handy.

Literary Soulmate:
Virgo

Sagittarius and Virgo both have a "my way or the highway" attitude that could cause them to clash. But when it comes to reading, they might just find they're on the same highway. Both like to see comprehensive, thoughtful world building and a chance to escape the mundane through thrilling books. They can also bond over their shared pet peeve of typos, plot holes, and inconsistencies they can't let go.

Famous Sagittarius Authors:
• Ann Patchett—December 2: Patchett's writing across place, time, and genre shows that a Sagittarius will always keep you on your toes.

• Sandra Cisneros—
December 20:

A classic Sagittarius straight shooter, Cisneros plays with form while encompassing social critiques and breaking taboos.

Reading Recommendations

• *Malagash* by Joey Comeau

When Sunday's father is dying, she wants to keep him alive forever—and she does so by recording his voice, over and over and over. Her plan is to release the recordings over the internet as a virus so he'll never die but expand and expand, instead. This is an unpredictable, heartfelt story of grief, loss, and the ways in which those who are in mourning will seek to preserve a loved one's memory. Sagittarius, chances are you'll be wondering if you can leave your legacy out there in the virtual world after your time comes to an end. How can you travel perpetually through the future?

• *The Third Rainbow Girl: The Long Life of a Double Murder in Appalachia* by Emma Copley Eisenberg

Let's travel to 1980, Pocono County, West Virginia. This true-crime tale will absolutely bring you somewhere new and complex, while taking you on an adventure to uncover who killed two middle-class, outsider girls in an isolated area. Vicky and Nancy hitchhiked to a festival known as the Rainbow Gathering, but they never made it. What unravels is a story of Appalachia, privilege, and what both outsiders and insiders think they know about a place's reputation. This book is one you'll love, Sagittarius, not just for these elements but also because it begs the debate of why we need to analyze our obsessions with death, crime, and rural America.

- *We Ride Upon Sticks* by Quan Barry

Because you love things that are different, you're going to fall madly for this story of the unexpected rise of the 1989 Danvers High field hockey team. Laced with humor, witchcraft, and a wide range of perspectives, this is a romp. You will cheer for a team who had no hopes of success just a year ago, but who found it via a photo of Emilio Estévez, eschewing femininity, and through the magical forces of Salem, Massachusetts's ancestry. The wordplay in this book will delight and surprise, as will the '80s-soaked pop culture references.

- *Blindspot: Hidden Biases of Good People* by Mahzarin R. Banaji and Anthony G. Greenwald

No matter how much of a straight shooter you are, Sagittarius, you've got what the authors of this book call "blind spots": a part of your brain that houses hidden, unconscious, and damaging biases. Learn how your perceptions of social groups shape the way you think about other people's abilities and character by unpacking the cultural attitudes we all carry with us, conscious or not. You're loved by others for being honest and true, and unpacking your beliefs and snap judgments about others will only make you more trustworthy. Looking inward can be hard for you, but it's always worth the journey.

- *Things You Can Only See When You Slow Down* by Haemin Sunim
Patience is not your biggest virtue, but it's not impossible to work on in your life. Sunim is a Buddhist teacher, and his short collection of meditative insights will give you a lot to chew on. You can certainly read this one cover to cover, absorbing everything as quickly as possible, but that'd run counter to the point. Pick it up and read sections bit by bit, considering how you can incorporate the lessons on being present and slowing down when it comes to passion, love, rest, the future, and more, in a mindful way. Bonus: You can give yourself space to argue and disagree with the ideas with which you disagree and examine why you hold those beliefs.

- *Several People Are Typing* by Calvin Kasulke
You love a fresh perspective, Sagittarius, and chances are you've never read a book set inside Slack. Yes, *inside* the digital workspace. Gerald's been uploaded to the company Slack and while everyone at work believes it to be a giant gag, it's not. When he enlists his coworker and friend to help him out—literally—even more office absurdity ensues. This is a darkly humorous read about office culture and it's sure to be one you'll love debating the meaning of with other readers. You'll also be firm in deciding what you'd do in Gerald's situation.

- *Blue Highways* by William Least Heat-Moon

Least-Heat Moon's classic American travelog might test your patience, but it's well worth it. You'll travel with the Osage-enrolled author through the highways of America, experiencing life in the places that interstates have bypassed. Discover stories of small towns, big dreams, the people within them, and, of course, adventures to places you may never have known existed. Take your time with this read, and if you find yourself enraptured, know there are two other stand-alone companion titles as well.

Further Reading

- *Joyful: The Surprising Power of Ordinary Things to Create Extraordinary Happiness* by Ingrid Fetell Lee

- *Nomadland: Surviving America in the Twenty-First Century* by Jessica Bruder
- *The Memory Police* by Yōko Ogawa
- *The Yellow House* by Sarah M. Broom
- *Wild Life: Dispatches From a Childhood of Baboons and Button-Downs* by Keena Roberts

Capricorn
(December 22–January 19)

—•——•——•—

ELEMENT: Earth

QUALITY: Cardinal

RULING PLANET: Saturn

SYMBOL: The Sea Goat

The Basics:

Every Capricorn has something to prove, and they won't rest until they've shown everyone what they're capable of accomplishing. As a cardinal earth sign, Capricorns love to take charge and win while playing by the rules. They may come across as overly serious or power hungry. But much like their symbol, the sea goat, they're all business at first glance and delightfully weird once you get to know them.

Capricorns love a business card more than any other sign, both handing them out and receiving them. Their social life is often driven by what connections and favors they can utilize, making them prolific networkers. They value tradition, loyalty, and hard work, but they also love to let loose and celebrate a big win.

As friends, Capricorns want to see you thrive, and they can always call in a favor with someone to help you out. However, they can struggle to relate to people who are quite different from them. In love, Capricorns are looking for stability, trustworthiness, and someone who can keep up with them socially and professionally. The sea goats are incredibly passionate about and dedicated to their jobs; they make excellent managers and leaders.

Capricorn Reading Life:

Because everything they do is in pursuit of a goal, Capricorns read primarily to learn, grow, or sometimes show off. They're some of the biggest fans of the self-help and business genres. When it comes to fiction, they may be guilty of choosing books based on what will look most impressive to others. But on the rare occasion when a Capricorn reads to relax, they love escaping with science fiction, fantasy, or romance. Capricorns see themselves in protagonists willing to do anything to get what they want.

In the bookish world, you'll find Capricorns setting ambitious reading goals and networking with other readers by comparing the longest books they've read. They love a book club, particularly ones with people they respect professionally and socially. Their bookshelves are full of textbooks, inspirational self-help books, and a few books they find "impressive" for conversation starters.

Reading for Growth:

Honestly, it's hard to recommend a self-help book to a Capricorn, because they've already read and absorbed them all. Books about getting ahead in business and influencing people are particular favorites. But to balance their inherent seriousness, books about letting loose and work-life balance may be helpful. As they can be a bit hardheaded, Capricorns could

also learn from books about being open to other perspectives and changing their minds.

Literary Soulmate: Aries

Capricorn and Aries tend to either love or hate each other, as their competitiveness and drive can lead either to mutual respect or to an intense rivalry. But when it comes to reading, both love nothing more than comparing the statuses of their reading goals and enormous TBRs. Both also love a strong protagonist with something to prove.

Famous Capricorn Authors:
- Stephenie Meyer— December 24:
Meyer's Capricorn sun sign might have helped her turn a good idea into a bestselling series and an impressive business.

Haruki Murakami—January 12: Murakami's prolific body of work shows his determination and drive, and his writing, much like the sea goat, is a little surreal.

Reading Recommendations

• *Genuine Fraud* by E. Lockhart Capricorns have a special appreciation for a ruthless, stop-at-nothing protagonist, and this thriller fits that bill with chilling, twisty perfection. Imogen Sokoloff lives at a fancy resort in Cabo San Lucas, Mexico, where she spends her days working out and regaling other guests about that time she got kicked out of Stanford. Except Imogen isn't really Imogen. She's Jule, the real Imogen is dead, and Jule is on the run from someone or something. Get comfortable with a little bit of confusion as each chapter reveals more and more about the last year in Jule's life, building up to an end that may leave you staring off into space.

• *White Ivy* by Susie Yang Ivy was taught by her grandmother to use her mild appearance for cover in stealing from yard sales and secondhand shops. But the jig is up when Ivy's mother finds out about their schemes and promptly sends Ivy off to China. Years later, now back in Boston, Ivy runs into the sister of Gideon Speyer, the golden boy from a wealthy political family and former object of Ivy's obsession. Ivy sees the meeting as fate, and before long she's reeling Gideon in at lavish parties and island getaways. Just when everything Ivy wants is right at her fingertips, a ghost from her past resurfaces and threatens to undo it all. But Ivy isn't ready to let that happen; she'll get what she wants, no matter the cost.

• *Just Work: Get Sh*t Done, Fast & Fair* by Kim Scott

So you've read all the buzzy business books and latest self-help, Capricorn. But how often do you put that knowledge to meaningful use in creating a more just workplace? Chances are, there's still lots to learn from Kim Scott's latest, a guide for recognizing, attacking, and eliminating workplace injustice. She provides a helpful framework for inviting true collaboration, respect, and inclusivity at work.

• *Boyfriend Material* by Alexis Hall

For the Capricorn who likes to unwind with a little romance, here's a delightful one between two lovebirds with a lot riding on a fake relationship. Luc O'Donnell is thrown back into the public eye when his in-and-out-of-rehab rockstar dad plans a comeback. When a compromising photo from a night out lands Luc in hot water at work, his boss orders him to find a nice, normal, fake boyfriend to help clean up his image. Luc's friends suggest straight-laced, squeaky-clean barrister Oliver for the role, and Oliver surprisingly agrees to the arrangement for work-related image issues of his own. They appear to have tragically little in common, but the more time they spend together . . . insert body roll here.

- *You Are Your Best Thing: Vulnerability, Shame Resilience, and the Black Experience* by Tarana Burke and Brené Brown

Me Too movement founder Tarana Burke and author Brené Brown were exchanging home decor ideas one day when Tarana asked if Brené could jump on a call. Brené expected more wallpaper and paint sample chat but was met with something much more serious: Tarana confessed that as a Black woman, she often struggled to see herself in Brené's work. Tarana suggested working together on a book about the Black experience with vulnerability and shame resilience, and that's how *You Are Your Best Thing* was born. The impressive list of contributors (Kiese Laymon, Imani Perry, Laverne Cox, Jason Reynolds, Austin Channing Brown, and more) will satisfy a Capricorn's love of an "impressive" read that invites reflection and difficult conversations.

- *The Secret History* by Donna Tartt

You love a conversation starter and an impressive page count, so let's talk about *The Secret History*. Set at a swanky New England college, this dark academia classic follows a group of eccentric misfits taking a classics course that's almost certainly (hopefully?) unlike any college course you've ever heard of. Under the tutelage and very loose supervision of their charismatic professor, the students start to experiment with the boundaries of morality. One night changes everything, and the aftermath is, shall we say . . . messy. We know you love a protagonist who'll do anything to get what they want. Here's a whole cast of characters to scratch that itch.

- *Transcendent Kingdom* by Yaa Gyasi

Gifty is a Ghanian American PhD candidate studying depression and addiction by observing reward-seeking behavior in mice. This work is personal for Gifty, who was just a kid when her brother became addicted to Oxycontin after a basketball injury and then died of an overdose. Gifty is trying so hard to find answers to these big, difficult questions through science, to make sense of the depth of her family's loss. But more and more she finds herself pulled in by the allure of salvation offered by the faith she thought she wanted nothing to do with. Gifty's relationship with that faith and with her mother will open up space for reflection on the power that comes with openness to changing one's mind.

Further Reading

- *Black Leopard, Red Wolf* by Marlon James

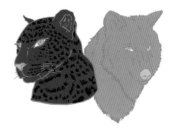

- *Chilling Effect* by Valerie Valdes
- *God Land: A Story of Faith, Loss, and Renewal in Middle America* by Lyz Lenz
- *How to Change Your Mind: What the New Science of Psychedelics Teaches Us About Consciousness, Dying, Addiction, Depression, and Transcendence* by Michael Pollan
- *The Incendiaries* by R.O. Kwon

Aquarius

(January 20–February 18)

ELEMENT: Air

QUALITY: Fixed

RULING PLANETS: Uranus and Saturn

SYMBOL: The Water Bearer

The Basics:

Aquarius has a bit of a reputation as the free-spirited hippie of the zodiac. That's partially because of their passionate desire to make the world a better place, and partially because of their disinterest in fitting social norms. As an air sign, Aquarius is intellectual, curious, and a bit distant at times. They are represented by the water bearer, symbolizing their desire to nurture and improve the world around them.

In the life cycle of the zodiac, Aquarius has the wisdom of old age and a bit of impatience for youth's superficiality. Their connection to the universe gives them a bit of a psychic or otherworldly sense. They are often seen as visionaries, eccentric weirdos, or both.

As friends, Aquarians can be a bit aloof, but will always have the most fascinating midnight conversations with you. In love, it's hard to get truly close to an Aquarius, but once you do, they'll do anything for you. Aquarians need passion and intellectual stimulation in their careers or they will quickly lose interest.

Aquarius Reading Life:

Aquarius reads for a window into another world or unique perspective. They especially love books that play with form or buck tradition. Fantasy and graphic novels are favorites, as well as poetry and creative memoir. The water bearer will read anything that makes them think and finds a way to surprise them.

You can find an Aquarius buying a bizarre combination of books at an independent bookstore or fundraising for their local library. They're also the first to sign up for a poetry open mic night. Their bookshelves are overflowing with books to help them change the world and to keep them thinking.

Reading for Growth:

Aquarius is naturally drawn to books about activism, social justice, and changing the world. They may be less interested in books about adulting and getting their life in order, but it might be a good idea to read them anyway. As Aquariases tend to never feel like they're doing enough to make a difference, they should consider lessons on accepting their limitations.

Literary Soulmate:

Leo

Aquarius's air and Leo's fire elements make them a fairly compatible pairing. When it comes to books, they've both got a soft spot for a plucky protagonist fighting to save the world. They can agree on fantasy, sci-fi, comics, memoir, and history books, particularly ones with badass heroes.

Famous Aquarius Authors:

• Elizabeth Acevedo—February 15:
Poetic AND forward-thinking AND breaking some traditions along the way? Big Aquarius vibes.

• Toni Morrison—February 18:
In true Aquarius fashion, Morrison was never afraid to speak her mind and used her gifts to make the world a better place.

Reading Recommendations

• *Life on Mars* by Tracy K. Smith

Quench that thirst for poetry with a Pulitzer Prize—winning writer, Aquariuses. Tracy K. Smith has graced us with a poetry collection that is as unique as it is genre bending. Smith takes a science-fictional approach to questions about human existence, melds the personal with the speculative, and explores intimate and historic events. Let this poet be your guide on a journey through space, pop culture, tragic events, and grief. The deep-thinking Aquarius will appreciate Smith's keen commentary on humanity and critical approach to some of the biggest headlines of recent history.

- *On Earth We're Briefly Gorgeous* by Ocean Vuong
Aquariuses in search of the unconventional, the poetic, and the personal should seek out Ocean Vuong. In Vuong's debut novel, the poet looks to the epistolary form to produce a novel that is a letter from a son to his mother. The correspondence unspools a Vietnam-centered family history and explores everything from race and class to masculinity. As in James Baldwin's *The Fire Next Time*, complex, urgent, and difficult subject matter is framed by the gentle and heartfelt act of writing a letter to a loved one. *On Earth We're Briefly Gorgeous* will satisfy the Aquarius's longing for awareness and delight them with a refreshing approach to timely topics.

• *The Sum of Us: What Racism Costs Everyone and How We Can Prosper Together* by Heather McGhee

For the Aquarius determined to make the world a better place, to emphasize the importance of community, and to uphold the benefits of sharing the wealth, look to American political commentator and strategist Heather McGhee and her nonfiction exploration of inequality. *The Sum of Us* challenges readers to take a critical look at the American economy and whom it's failed. She addresses how inequality has affected people of color and how a zero-sum paradigm also negatively impacts white people. For McGhee, the journey to understanding is personal, and she's here to take you, thoughtful Aquarius, with her down the path toward equity and a Solidarity Dividend.

• *Bored and Brilliant: How Spacing Out Can Unlock Your Most Productive and Creative Self* by Manoush Zomorodi

Okay, Aquarius. I know you'd rather take a big look at the world around you and devote your minutes to making a big impact, but maybe it's time to take a deep breath and a walk in the park. Before you plug in your headphones and push play on your favorite activism podcast, consider Manoush Zomorodi's suggestion to tune in by tuning out. In *Bored and Brilliant*, the creator of the WNYC podcast *Note to Self* urges us to take the time to sit around and let our minds run, instead of trying to squeeze creative and productive thinking into a noisy room. If you, dear Aquarius, are hesitant about adulting books, this is your gentle entry point.

• *American Love Story*
by Adriana Herrera

Hey, Aquarius. Worried that your love life will get in the way of public service? Think again, and read this queer romance about a Haitian-born professor and activist and an assistant district attorney. Activist Patrice Denis may not be able to forget steamy nights with DA Easton Archer, but he's not about to let that golden boy distract him from justice-seeking. Patrice and Easton come from two different worlds, but rising tensions between the community and local law enforcement are taking them on a collision course. They might have to work together to get through this one.

• *Vita Nostra* by Maryna and Serhiy Dyachenko, translated by Julia Meitov Hersey

Get ready to get weird, Aquarius, because *Vita Nostra* is like nothing you've read before. This deeply metaphysical dark academia read following a brilliant and driven young student by the name of Sasha Samokhina will transport you to the Institute of Special Technologies where nothing is as it seems. The stakes are high for Sasha, who has to use her intellect and fierce ambition to succeed in her studies, or see her family face dire consequences. Wise beyond her years, Sasha is a protagonist who will speak to every Aquarius, and her journey will satisfy readers in search of the otherworldly.

- *Emma* by Jane Austen

Call this recommendation a gentle nudge to turn that attentive eye and urge to do good inward, Aquarius. In this beloved classic, well-meaning yet intrusive Emma Woodhouse sees room for improvement everywhere around her. From her neighbors to her family to her new bestie Harriet Smith—anyone and everyone needs Emma's help, as far as Emma is concerned. While the Aquarius might balk at being compared to a spoiled socialite, Austen's tale reminds us to take a step back, take a deep breath, and examine our own lives and motives before we go on a great quest to tackle everyone else's problems.

Further Reading

- *Drop the Ball: Achieving More by Doing Less* by Tiffany Dufu
- *Gingerbread* by Helen Oyeyemi
- *My Favorite Thing Is Monsters* by Emil Ferris
- *The Space Between Worlds* by Micaiah Johnson
- *Two Old Women: An Alaskan Legend of Betrayal, Courage and Survival* by Velma Wallis

Pisces

(February 19–March 20)

ELEMENT: Water

QUALITY: Mutable

RULING PLANETS: Neptune and Jupiter

SYMBOL: Two Fish

The Basics:

Pisces have super-power levels of empathy and emotional intelligence. They're the oldest and most mature sign of the zodiac, and they have the compassion and sensitivity of a water sign. As eternal dreamers and optimists, they can also get a bit lost in the clouds. Pisces are represented by two fish swimming in opposite directions, showing their ability to go with the flow but also their constant pull between fantasy and reality.

Innately creative, Pisces are artistic and especially connected to music. Their intuition and ability to read others gives them a touch of psychic energy. Pisces care deeply about other people and make great caretakers. They can adjust to any social situation but can also be easily influenced by the people around them. Be gentle with Pisces, because they're special creatures you'll want to keep in your life.

Pisces are the most caring, thoughtful friends you can ever hope to have. You may need to remind them to care for themselves sometimes, too. They're romantics at heart who long for deep emotional connection, but their openness can mean they get hurt easily. At work, Pisces care more about people than profit. They make excellent health-care workers, teachers, counselors, and anything else that requires sensitivity and emotional intelligence.

Pisces Reading Life:

Emotional and creative narratives are favorites of Pisces. They tend toward books that are deeply human, heartfelt, and authentic. As eternal optimists and romantics, Pisces also love a good love story or anything that leaves them feeling hopeful. Vulnerable memoir and poetry speak to them on a deep level.

Pisces give excellent bookish gifts and guide deep, honest conversations in book clubs. They're not at all ashamed of their bookshelf full of romance novels and will proudly tell you that everyone should read whatever books make them happy, regardless of what other people think.

Reading for Growth:

Pisces' vulnerability and sensitivity opens them up to easily getting hurt, so books about recovering from pain and not taking rejection too personally may be useful. They may also benefit from reminders to practice self-care as much as they care for the people around them. But really, what can you teach the most emotionally intelligent sign of the zodiac?

Literary Soulmate: Libra

Pisces and Libra both have a tendency to put others before themselves, although they may go about it in different ways. When it comes to books, they can bond over their love of feel-good books and atmospheric writing that gives them all the right vibes. They also share a passion for creating the perfect comfy reading spot.

Famous Pisces Authors:

• Khaled Hosseini—March 4: Hosseini's emotional bestselling novels and advocacy on behalf of refugees show he's a classic Pisces empath.

• Glennon Doyle—March 20: Building a career writing books about compassion, valuing relationships, and self-love? That's as Pisces as it gets.

Reading Recommendations

- *The Book of Delights* by Ross Gay

It's so easy for a Pisces to get bogged down in All the Feelings, which is where Ross Gay comes in. In this joy of a collection, he cele-brates something each day—from the mundane to the spiritual to the absurd—that brings him delight. Whether you dip your toes in or dive in headfirst, this book is a balm for the soul and an affirma-tion of all the wonders of living in this world, being in community with others, and finding the bright spot in any day.

- *Redemption in Indigo* by Karen Lord

Paama is a heroine after a Pisces's heart: She loves to care for others, but she's also done being taken advantage of by her foolish husband. Then a trick-ster god gets involved, granting Paama the power to manipulate the world around her, and super-natural hijinks ensue! Based on a Senegalese folktale, this retelling uses the singsong cadence of oral storytelling and Lord's own way with words to weave a story that is emotionally honest, funny, and warm-hearted from start to finish. It's also a must-read for anyone who has ever tried to make order from chaos.

- The Wayfarers series by Becky Chambers

Relationships are at the heart of any Pisces' life, and the families of origin and choice in Becky Chambers's Wayfarers series are one of the highlights of these cozy sci-fi novels. Whether doing interstellar construction work with a plucky crew, finding identity on a personal quest, or stuck in a bio-dome with strangers, these characters are all just trying to do their best. Sure, they make mistakes, but they also care for each other along the way, and journeying with them is worth every minute

spent reading. Permission to come aboard: Granted!

- *Year of Yes* by Shonda Rhimes

When you feel things so deeply, it's hard to know where the right lines are for protecting your-self as well as giving to others. And believe it or not, Shonda Rhimes was living that problem. Overextended in some ways and too afraid of failing to stretch her-self in others, Rhimes spent a year learning to say "Yes!" (and "No!") for herself, breaking the patterns that no longer served her. There are lots of great anecdotes about a career in Hollywood alongside real-talk about life, and Rhimes is a funny and wise guide to finding your own best boundaries.

• *Girls Made of Snow and Glass* by Melissa Bashardoust

Want a little more fantasy with your life lessons? This gorgeous retelling of "Snow White" is exactly what you're looking for. Mina and Lynet have each been shaped by their fathers, for better and—mostly—for worse, and their interactions with each other are heading in a direction neither wants to go. As they figure out who they are without the toxic narratives that have been forced upon them, they also find each other anew. A must-read for any Pisces who needs to refocus on themselves and on the people who will give back as much as they receive.

• *Lord of Scoundrels* by Loretta Chase

You love a happy ending, and you love a classic romance—and *Lord of Scoundrels* has both and how. It's also stood the test of time, becoming a classic you can reread over and over. Jessica Trent is a heroine for the ages: feisty, no-nonsense, and ready to fix her wastrel brother's life. Lord Dain is a brooder and suspicious of her motives, and the fire between the two of them will have you speed turning every page. This is for the Pisces who loves a story about family, true love, and unlikely soulmates. In other words, every Pisces!

• *Middlemarch* by George Eliot If Dorothea isn't a Pisces, then no one is. She lives to make a difference in this world and to be of service to others, and it leads her into a marriage that proves . . . less than ideal, let's say. This classic, while hefty, will surprise you with how quickly it sucks you in. As you watch Dorothea and the other characters find that their emotions often lead them astray before leading them back to the right path, consider how often your own feelings have gotten you both in and out of trouble, and take comfort!

Further Reading

• *Crystal Clear: Reflections on Extraordinary Talismans for*

Everyday Life by Jaya Saxena
• *How to Write an Autobiographical Novel* by Alexander Chee
• *Let's Talk About Love* by Claire Kann
• *So Lucky* by Nicola Griffith
• *Travel Light* by Naomi Mitchison

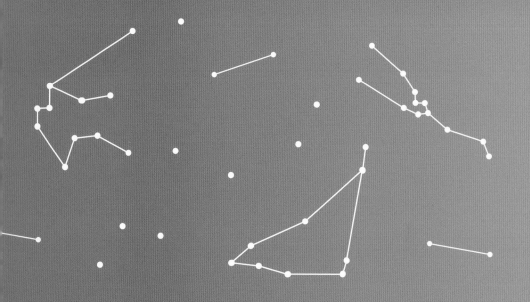

LIBRARY

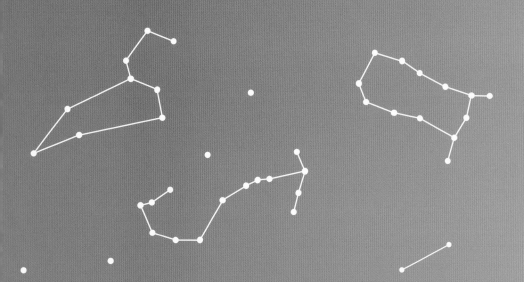

Astrology Basics

- *The Inner Sky: How to Make Wiser Choices for a More Fulfilling Life* by Steven Forrest

A tried and true classic of astrology texts, this won the PAI (Professional Astrologers Incorporated) Award when it was originally published in 1985. Learn the basics of astrology, then work through a step-by-step process to make sense of your signs.

- *On the Heavenly Spheres* by Helena Avelar and Luis Ribeiro

Develop a deep understanding of astrological concepts along with practical methods for applying them in your life. Avelar and Ribeiro eschew formulaic instructions in favor of teaching readers how to build an astrology practice that works for their individual needs.

- *The Complete Guide to Astrology: Understanding Yourself, Your Signs, and Your Birth Chart* by Louise Edington

This recent addition to the universe of astrology books offers in-depth introductions to the foundational concepts of astrology and walks readers through creating and reading their birth charts. Come for the comprehensive overview, stay for the inclusive, nonbinary approach that makes this book unique among its peers.

- *You Were Born For This: Astrology for Radical Self-Acceptance* by Chani Nicholas

What if your horoscope were less of a prediction about who you are and more of a tool for understanding yourself and guiding personal growth? If that sounds good, this book packed with journal prompts, reflections, affirmations, and three keys to applying the wisdom of your birth chart is for you.

- *Astro Poets: Your Guides to the Zodiac* by Alex Dimitrov and Dorothea Lasky

This astrology primer from the Twitter sensations is perfect for the extremely online twenty-first-century reader. Apply astrology to life, love, work, and friendships, and laugh along with the unique voice of the Astro Poets.

- *Postcolonial Astrology: Reading the Planets Through Capital, Power, and Labor* by Alice Sparkly Kat

Astrology isn't just about personal transformation. This radical new entry to the pantheon of astrology texts guides readers to use astrology as a tool for political work, social justice, and community connection.

Books by Sign

Aries

Warcross by Marie Lu

Haikyu!! series by Haruichi Furudate, translated by Adrienne Beck

The Regional Office Is Under Attack! by Manuel Gonzales

How to Do Nothing: Resisting the Attention Economy by Jenny Odell

Radical Acceptance: Embracing Your Life with the Heart of a Buddha by Tara Brach

Dead Dead Girls by Nekesa Afia

Four Thousand Weeks: Time Management for Mortals by Oliver Burkeman

Binti by Nnedi Okorafor

Dumplin' by Julie Murphy

How to Live Safely in a Science Fictional Universe by Charles Yu

The Girls I've Been by Tess Sharpe

The Year of the Witching by Alexis Henderson

Taurus

The Broken Earth series by N.K. Jemisin

Northern Light by Kazim Ali

The Cheffe by Marie NDiaye, translated by Jordan Stump

Brave, Not Perfect: How Celebrating Imperfection Helps You Live Your Best, Most Joyful Life by Reshma Saujani

Spaceman of Bohemia by Jaroslav Kalfař

The Black Count by Tom Reiss

Wintering by Katherine May

Avatar, The Last Airbender: The Rise of Kyoshi by F.C. Yee

Pilgrim at Tinker Creek by Annie Dillard

Believers: Making a Life at the End of the World by Lisa Wells

The Language of Baklava by Diana Abu-Jaber

Trejo's Tacos: Recipes and Stories from L.A. by Danny Trejo

Gemini

Clap When You Land by Elizabeth Acevedo

Tiny Beautiful Things: Advice on Love and Life from Dear Sugar by Cheryl Strayed

Everfair by Nisi Shawl

The Checklist Manifesto: How to Get Things Right by Atul Gawande

The Body Is Not an Apology: The Power of Radical Self-Love by Sonya Renee Taylor

The Strange Case of Dr. Jekyll and Mr. Hyde by Robert Louis Stevenson

The Chosen and the Beautiful by Nghi Vo

Adaptation by Malinda Lo

Falling in Love with Hominids by Nalo Hopkinson

Strong Female Protagonist by Brennan Lee Mulligan, illustrated by Molly Ostertag

The Summer We Got Free by Mia McKenzie

The Truth About Stories: A Native Narrative by Thomas King

Cancer

Girl Woman Other by Bernardine Evaristo

The Switch by Beth O'Leary

Spirit Run: A 6,000-Mile Marathon Through North America's Stolen Land by Noé Álvarez

When Things Fall Apart: Heart Advice for
Difficult Times by Pema Chödrön

The Magical Language of Others by E.J. Koh

The Ones We're Meant to Find by Joan He

Honey Girl by Morgan Rogers

Howl's Moving Castle by Diana Wynne Jones

The Prey of Gods by Nicky Drayden

Thanks for Waiting: The Joy (& Weirdness) of
Being a Late Bloomer by Doree Shafir

The Night Watchman by Louise Erdrich

The Pretty One: On Life, Pop Culture,
Disability, and Other Reasons to Fall in
Love with Me by Keah Brown

Leo

Shuri: The Search for Black Panther
by Nnedi Okorafor (writer) and
Leonardo Romero (artist)

The Queen of the Night by Alexander Chee

The Rib King by Ladee Hubbard

Klara and the Sun by Kazuo Ishiguro

The Power of Vulnerability: Teachings on
Authenticity, Connection, and Courage
by Brené Brown

Anne of Green Gables by Lucy Maud
Montgomery

Mem by Bethany Morrow

Not Your Sidekick by C.B. Lee

Nothing to See Here by Kevin Wilson

Quiet: The Power of Introverts in a World
That Can't Stop Talking by Susan Cain

These Ghosts Are Family by Maisy Card

Uprooted by Naomi Novik

Virgo

Everything I Never Told You by Celeste Ng

Fingersmith by Sarah Waters

Why Fish Don't Exist: A Story of Loss, Love,
and the Hidden Order of Life by Lulu
Miller

The Pursuit of Perfect: How to Stop Chasing
Perfection and Start Living a Richer,
Happier Life by Tal Ben-Shahar

See No Stranger: A Memoir and Manifesto of
Revolutionary Love by Valerie Kour

The Lord of the Rings trilogy by J.R.R.
Tolkien

Rest: Why You Get More Done When You
Work Less by Alex Soojung-Kim Pang

A Wizard of Earthsea by Ursula K. Le Guin

Butter Honey Pig Bread by Francesca
Ekwuyasi

Stamped from the Beginning: The Definitive
History of Racist Ideas in America
by Ibram X. Kendi

The Argonauts by Maggie Nelson

The Hidden Keys by André Alexis

Libra

Mexican Gothic by Silvia Moreno-Garcia

A Master of Djinn by P. Djèlí Clark

The Compton Cowboys: The New
Generation of Cowboys in America's
Urban Heartland by Walter
Thompson-Hernández

Hana Khan Carries On by Uzma Jalaluddin

Over the Top: A Raw Journey to Self-Love
by Jonathan Van Ness

Practical Magic by Alice Hoffman

Hill House Living: The Art of Creating a Joyful Life by Paula Sutton

Everything's Trash, but It's Okay by Phoebe Robinson

Night Theater by Vikram Paralkar

Survival of the Thickest by Michelle Buteau

The Forest of Stolen Girls by June Hur

The Only Good Indians by Stephen Graham Jones

Scorpio

Our Kind of Cruelty by Araminta Hall

The Gilded Wolves by Roshani Chokshi

Women and Other Monsters: Building a New Mythology by Jess Zimmerman

Once Upon a Quinceañera by Monica Gomez-Hira

Notes from a Young Black Chef by Kwame Onwuachi with Joshua David Stein

The Count of Monte Cristo by Alexandre Dumas

The Road Trip by Beth O'Leary

A Tip for the Hangman by Allison Epstein

My Sister, the Serial Killer by Oyinkan Braithwaite

The Five: The Untold Lives of the Women Killed by Jack the Ripper by Hallie Rubenhold

The Wild Woman's Guide to Traveling the World by Kristin Rockaway

Sagittarius

Malagash by Joey Cameau

The Third Rainbow Girl: The Long Life of a Double Murder in Appalachia by Emma Copley Eisenberg

We Ride Upon Sticks by Quan Barry

Blindspot: Hidden Biases of Good People by Mahzarin R. Banaji and Anthony G. Greenwald

Things You Can Only See When You Slow Down by Haemin Sunim

Several People Are Typing by Calvin Kasulke

Blue Highways by William Least Heat-Moon

Joyful: The Surprising Power of Ordinary Things to Create Extraordinary Happiness by Ingrid Fetell Lee

Nomadland: Surviving America in the Twenty-First Century by Jessica Bruder

The Memory Police by Yōko Ogawa

The Yellow House by Sarah M. Brown

Wild Life: Dispatches from a Childhood of Baboons and Button-Downs by Keena Roberts

Capricorn

Genuine Fraud by E. Lockhart

White Ivy by Susie Yang

*Just Work: Get Sh*t Done, Fast & Fair* by Kim Scott

Boyfriend Material by Alexis Hall

You Are Your Best Thing: Vulnerability, Shame Resilience, and the Black Experience by Tarana Burke and Brené Brown

The Secret History by Donna Tartt

Transcendent Kingdom by Yao Gyasi

Black Leopard, Red Wolf by Marlon James

Chilling Effect by Valerie Valdes

God Land: A Story of Faith, Loss, and Renewal in Middle America by Lyz Lenz

How to Change Your Mind: What the New Science of Psychedelics Teaches Us About Consciousness, Dying, Addiction, Depression, and Transcendence by Michael Pollan

The Incendiaries by R.O. Kwan

Aquarius

Life on Mars by Tracy K. Smith

On Earth We Were Briefly Gorgeous by Ocean Vuong

The Sum of Us: What Racism Costs Everyone and How We Can Prosper Together by Heather McGhee

Bored and Brilliant: How Spacing Out Can Unlock Your Most Productive and Creative Self by Manoush Zamarodi

American Love Story by Adriana Herrera

Vita Nostro by Maryna and Serhiy Dyachenko, translated by Julia Meitov Hersey

Emma by Jane Austen

Drop the Ball: Achieving More by Doing Less by Tiffany Dufu

Gingerbread by Helen Oyeyemi

My Favorite Thing Is Monsters by Emil Ferris

The Space Between Worlds by Micaiah Johnson

Two Old Women: An Alaskan Legend of Betrayal, Courage and Survival by Velma Wallis

Pisces

The Book of Delights by Ross Gay

Redemption in Indigo by Karen Lord

The Wayfarers series by Becky Chambers

Year of Yes by Shonda Rhimes

Girls Made of Snow and Glass by Melissa Bashardoust

Lord of Scoundrels by Loretta Chase

Middlemarch by George Eliot

Crystal Clear: Reflections on Extraordinary Talismans for Everyday Life by Jaya Saxena

How to Write an Autobiographical Novel by Alexander Chee

Let's Talk About Love by Claire Kann

So Lucky by Nicola Griffith

Travel Light by Naomi Mitchison

ACKNOWLEDGMENTS

Thank you to the Book Riot team, including Kelly Jensen, who first suggested that we do something fun with astrology; Sharifah Williams, Vanessa Diaz, Susie Dumond, Danika Ellis, Erica Ezeifedi, and Jenn Northington. To our editor, Meredith Clark, and the crew at Abrams for understanding the Book Riot magic and helping bring these ideas to life. And to the Book Riot community who have been expanding the literary conversation with us since 2011, and without whom none of this would be possible.

Editor: Meredith A. Clark
Managing Editor: Mike Richards
Designer: Jenice Kim
Production Manager: Sarah Masterson Hally

Library of Congress Control Number: 2022932897

ISBN: 978-1-4197-5887-4
eISBN: 978-1-64700-551-1

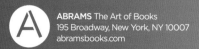

ABRAMS The Art of Books
195 Broadway, New York, NY 10007
abramsbooks.com